THE SAVAGE ARSENAL

Business and Financial Literacy for the Everyday Hustler

By Joseph Grimes

grimetimeready.com

THE SAVAGE ARSENAL

Business and Financial Literacy for the Everyday Hustler

For permission requests, speaking engagements, bulk orders, or other inquiries, contact the author at: www.grimetimeready.com

ISBN (Paperback): 979-8-9954482-4-2

ISBN (eBook / ePub): 979-8-9954482-3-5

The information contained in this book is for educational and informational purposes only. The author is not a licensed financial advisor, attorney, accountant, or investment professional. Nothing in this book constitutes financial, legal, tax, or investment advice. Individual results will vary. The author makes no

First Edition, 2025

Printed in the United States of America

Grime Time Ready | grimetimeready.com | @grimetimeready

DEDICATION

This one is for my children, and for the mentees I may never meet.

The good news about books is that if they are any good, they have a tendency to stick around. I wrote this hoping it sticks around long enough to find the people who needed it before they even knew it existed, the ones still figuring it out, the ones just starting, the ones who never had anyone sit down and give them the whole picture.

This book is for you. I hope it does some good.

— Joseph Grimes

Table of Contents

Part Six — The Sales Blueprint

THE SAVAGE ARSENAL — FOREWORD

Before You Read This Book

"The system might be rigged. The deck might be stacked. But if you lose, it's still your fault."

I was twelve years old running a full operation out of my backpack. Pokémon cards, lollipops, whatever moved. I didn't know what a profit margin was. I just knew what sold, what didn't, and that if I wanted something I had to go get it, because nobody in my neighborhood was pulling kids aside to explain how credit works or why the difference between an asset and a liability is the difference between building wealth and financing someone else's.

I grew up in Orlando, in the kind of neighborhood where making it out was the exception. I say that with no self-pity attached because self-pity is expensive and I've never been able to afford it. What I could afford was attention. Paying attention to what worked, to who was winning and how, to what people in rooms I wasn't invited into were doing differently. Eventually I stopped waiting for an invitation and found my own way in.

They used to pick me up from my hood and drop me off in rich suburbs to sell candy door-to-door. I had about ten seconds at a stranger's door to make them trust me enough to open their wallet, and what I learned in those ten seconds nobody ever taught me in a classroom. People buy you before they buy the product. Confidence reads louder than your pitch. And "No" is just data. I took those same instincts to Verizon, a Fortune 50 company, put on the collared shirt, and did numbers most people on that floor had never seen. For two years straight I averaged 200 to 225 percent to target, and the only time I dropped to 175 was when the company changed direction, shifted the metrics, or threw all its weight behind a new product push. The average salesperson hit 95 to 100 percent. The good ones got excited about 130. And plenty of them got there the ugly way, leaning on aggressive, pushy tactics, selling people things they did not want just to hit a vanity number the company cared about. I went the other way. I focused on solving the actual problem in front of me and shrinking the chance that anything I sold ever came back as a return. I talked to every customer like they were my brother, my sister, my mother, my father, my grandmother. Then I gave them a real recommendation, backed by the reasons they had just handed me in the conversation we were having a few minutes earlier. The principles I learned selling candy at fourteen are the same ones that built my businesses, my credit score, and my investment portfolio as an adult.

I bought my first house at twenty-four without a bag of cash sitting around. I had discipline, sweat equity, and the willingness to figure out what I didn't know as fast as humanly possible. Every lesson I learned the hard way, I wrote down. This book is what happened when I put all of those lessons together.

The Savage Arsenal is six books in one and every single one of them is a weapon. I didn't write this to motivate you. Motivation is sugar and you don't need sugar, you need a system. That's exactly what this is.

We start with the Accountability Gap because that's where everything actually starts. If you skip that section and go straight to the business content, you will build on a cracked foundation and wonder why nothing holds. Read it even if you think you don't need it, and especially if you think you don't need it. After that we get into credit, and if your eyes just glazed over, understand that a bad credit score is a tax you pay every month on your car note, your mortgage, your business loans, and your future. We are closing that gap. Then we get into financial literacy: the real version. Assets versus liabilities. Cash flow over net worth. How the wealthy use the tax code legally to keep more of what they make while most people get taxed on the gross and wonder where their check went. Then we build the business, step by step, with the actual paperwork and the actual process and no gatekeeping. And if you don't have startup capital, we handle that too, because there are ten businesses in this book you can launch this weekend for under four hundred dollars. We close with the sale, because everything in your life is a sale, and if you can't sell you can't build.

I am not a guru. I don't have a yacht. I have an MBA, an 800-plus credit score, and three businesses, and I still run into walls. What I know for certain is that waiting on the system to change is the longest losing bet you can make, and the people who are actually building something aren't waiting on anything.

This book is for the everyday hustler who is tired of getting information in pieces and wants the whole picture in one place with no fluff and no gatekeeping. Everything I know, everything I've tested, and everything I've learned from winning and losing is in here.

Your Arsenal is loaded. Let's get to work.

Joseph Grimes

Author · Sales Leader · Everyday Hustler

PART ONE

The Accountability Gap

Why You're Failing and How to Take the Wheel

"The system might be rigged. The deck might be stacked. But if you lose, it's still your fault."

There is a version of your life that you have pictured. A version where the money is right, the stress is manageable, the people around you are solid, and you actually feel like you are moving forward instead of running in place. You have seen that version clearly enough to want it. The gap between that version and where you are standing right now is what this section is about.

Most people spend their entire lives explaining that gap instead of closing it. They have a reason for everything: the economy, their upbringing, the neighborhood, the boss, the system. And some of those reasons are legitimate. I am not going to stand here and tell you the system is fair, because it is not, and anyone who says otherwise has never had to fight for a seat at the table. But reasons do not pay your bills. They do not raise your kids. They do not build your business or fix your credit or get you out of bed at five in the morning when you do not feel like it. Reasons are comfortable, and comfort is the enemy of progress.

This section is going to be uncomfortable. That is intentional.

CHAPTER 1.1

Defining the Gap

The Accountability Gap is the distance between your intentions and your reality, and almost everyone has one. The size of yours is what determines the quality of your life.

You intend to be financially free, but your bank account says otherwise. You intend to be present for your family, but the hours you log somewhere else tell a different story. You intend to start the business, get healthy, fix the relationship, deal with the debt. And every year that passes, the intention stays exactly where it is while the reality moves further in the wrong direction. That distance is the gap. And the gap does not close on its own.

Psychologists call this the Locus of Control. People with an external locus of control believe that what happens to them is primarily determined by outside forces: luck, other people, the economy, circumstances. People with an internal locus of control believe they are the primary driver of their outcomes. The research on this is not subtle. People with an internal locus of control earn more, are healthier, have more stable relationships, and recover faster from setbacks. The external group spends a lot of time being right about how unfair things are, and not a lot of time winning.

The moment you place the cause of your situation outside of yourself, you have also placed the solution outside of yourself. If the economy is why you are broke, then you cannot be financially free until the economy changes. If your boss is why you are stuck, then you cannot move until your boss does. You have handed your future to someone else and called it honesty. That is not honesty. That is surrender with better vocabulary.

Taking ownership does not mean pretending the obstacles are not real. It means deciding that you are more powerful than they are. Those are two completely different things, and one of them gets you somewhere.

CHAPTER 1.2

The History

We have to talk about where this comes from, because the Accountability Gap does not appear out of nowhere. It is learned. It is inherited. And for a lot of people, it was handed to them by a world that failed them before they ever had a chance to fail themselves.

If you grew up in an environment where the adults around you were victims of circumstances they could not fully control, and many of them genuinely were, then victimhood becomes the framework you are handed for understanding the world. You watch people you love work hard and still lose, get cheated and stay cheated, try and fail in ways that seem to confirm that trying does not matter. And at some point, something in you decides that effort and outcome are not connected, so why bother connecting them.

That is not weakness. That is a rational response to an irrational environment. The problem is that you carry that response into a life where it no longer applies, and it becomes a cage you built yourself.

The communities hit hardest by this are the ones that have been systematically excluded from the wealth-building tools that everyone else takes for granted: homeownership, business loans, generational knowledge about money, fathers in the home. Those exclusions were real and they were deliberate, and the data on what happens to families when those foundations are stripped away is not ambiguous.

But I know this from my own life and from watching people come up from nothing: you can acknowledge all of that and still decide it does not get the final word. The history explains where you are. It does not have to dictate where you end up. Continuing a cycle because the cycle started before you were born is still a choice, and it is the most expensive choice you will ever make.

Understanding the history is not about assigning blame. It is about seeing clearly what you are working with and what you are working against, so you can build a plan that is honest about both.

CHAPTER 1.3

The Data on Dads

I grew up without a father in the house. My mother did everything she could, and I mean everything, but there are things she could not teach me about being a man because she had never been one. I had to learn in the mud. I made mistakes that a present father might have helped me avoid, and I spent years unlearning things I picked up from the wrong people because I was looking for a blueprint from anyone who seemed to have one.

I am not telling that story for sympathy. I am telling it because the data behind it is one of the most important and least discussed contributors to the Accountability Gap, and if we are going to have an honest conversation about why people fail to close it, we have to go here.

The numbers from the U.S. Census Bureau and the Department of Justice are not subtle about what happens when fathers are absent from the home.

85% of youths in prison come from fatherless homes.

2x more likely: boys without fathers end up incarcerated at twice the rate of those with present fathers.

71% more likely: girls without fathers become pregnant as teenagers at nearly triple the rate.

Higher rates of depression, anxiety, and academic failure across the board.

And the flip side of those numbers is just as clear. Young people with present, positive father figures are significantly more likely to graduate, stay out of the system, and build income that compounds over time into actual wealth. The father in the home is not just an emotional variable. He is an economic one.

If you are a man reading this, your presence is the single greatest investment you can make in your children's future. Not the sneakers you buy them. Not the birthday money. Your actual physical and emotional presence, consistently, over time. The research is unambiguous on this. When you leave, you are not just creating a void. You are statistically stacking the deck against your own kids in every area that matters.

And if you grew up without that presence yourself, the work is not to be angry about it forever. The work is to break the cycle by becoming what you needed. That is the most accountable thing a person can do with a wound: turn it into a weapon for the next generation instead of a reason to keep bleeding.

CHAPTER 1.4

The Cost of Zero Accountability

Lack of accountability is not a personality flaw you can afford to be casual about. It has a dollar amount attached to it. It has a health cost attached to it. It shows up in your relationships, your stress levels, your sleep, and your bank account, and it compounds the same way interest does, slowly at first, and then all at once.

Your credit score is the most literal example of this. A FICO score is a mathematical measurement of whether you keep your promises. Every time you said you would pay something and did not, the score went down. Every time you maxed out a card and ignored it, the score went down. The score does not care about your circumstances. It just tracks your behavior over time and assigns it a number. And that number will cost you or save you tens of thousands of dollars over the course of your life, depending on which side of 700 you sit on.

A 600 credit score on a thirty-year mortgage costs you somewhere between fifty and a hundred thousand dollars more in interest than a 720 does. On a car loan, you might pay eighteen percent interest while someone with better credit pays six. That difference is not small. That is the cost of the gap showing up in your finances, quietly, every single month, for years.

The health side of this is just as real. Chronic stress, the kind that comes from knowing you have problems you are not handling, is one of the most damaging things you can do to your body over time. The bills you are ignoring, the conversation you keep putting off, the thing you know you should do but haven't, all of it sits in your nervous system as low-grade stress that never fully goes away. People think stress is a feeling. It is also a physical condition, and it is slowly breaking down your body while you pretend the problem does not exist.

Then there is the mental cost. Procrastination creates anxiety. Not the other way around. When you know you are avoiding something that matters, your brain does not let you fully rest. It keeps sending signals that something is wrong, because something is wrong, and the only thing that turns off those signals is doing the thing. Avoidance feels like relief in the short term and torture in the long term. Accountability feels like discomfort in the short term and freedom in the long term. Most people pick the wrong one.

CHAPTER 1.5

The Fake Success Epidemic

Because so many of us grew up without mentors who could show us what real success looked like up close, we started modeling ourselves after whatever we could see. And what we could see was the surface. The car. The clothes. The watch. The Instagram grid. The appearance of having arrived, with no information about what it actually cost to get there or whether it was real at all.

This created an entire economy of performance. People spending money they do not have on things they do not need to impress people who are doing the exact same thing. Leasing luxury cars on incomes that cannot sustain them. Popping bottles in sections they financed on a credit card. Posting lifestyle content that has nothing to do with their actual net worth, which in many cases is negative.

The Pretender is not a bad person. The Pretender is a person who was never taught the difference between looking successful and being successful, and who chose the version that gets immediate validation because the other version takes years and nobody can see it happening. That is a human response to a broken framework. But it is still a losing strategy, and the bill always comes.

The person actually building something looks completely different. They drive a paid-off car until their assets generate enough cash flow to buy something better without touching their liquidity. They are not chasing attention. They are chasing ownership. They are not in competition with people on social media because they understand that someone else's highlight reel has nothing to do with their balance sheet. They protect their time and their energy the same way they protect their money, because they have figured out that all three are finite and all three compound.

The question is not which version looks better on a Saturday night. The question is which version you want your life to look like in ten years. Because both paths are available, and you are on one of them right now whether you chose it consciously or not.

CHAPTER 1.6

How to Fix It

Accountability is a skill, not a trait. You were not born with it or without it. You build it the same way you build anything, through deliberate practice, repeated over time, until it becomes automatic. Here is how you start.

The first step is the mirror audit, and it is the hardest one. Sit down with no distractions, no phone, no music, nothing, and write down everything in your life that is not where you want it to be. Your finances. Your health. Your relationships. Your career. Your habits. Everything that is honest, even the things that are embarrassing to admit. Then next to each one, write how you contributed to it being that way. Not how someone else contributed. How you did. This is not about self-punishment. It is about finding the levers that are actually in your control, because those are the only ones you can pull.

The second step is shifting your language, and this sounds small until you realize how much the words you use shape the way you think. Stop saying "I have to." Start saying "I choose to." Those two phrases feel identical on the surface and are completely different underneath. "I have to go to work" positions you as someone who is being acted upon. "I choose to go to work because it funds my next move" positions you as someone in control of their own decisions. You are the same person doing the same thing, but one version of you has agency and one version does not. Build the habit of speaking like the version that has agency.

The third step is the delayed gratification drill, and the research on this goes back decades. The ability to choose a larger future reward over a smaller immediate one is one of the strongest predictors of long-term success across income, health, and relationships. The way you build that muscle is the same way you build any muscle. You practice it in small doses until it gets easier. Skip the purchase you do not need. Save the money instead of spending it. Read instead of scrolling. Work out when you do not feel like it. None of these are about the specific action. They are about training your brain to prioritize the future version of you over the present one.

The fourth step is auditing your circle, and this one costs people relationships they are not ready to lose.

Your environment is not just physical. It is the people you spend the most time around, and those people are either pulling you toward the life you want or making it easier to stay where you are. If the people around you do not hold you to a standard, if they laugh at your ambition or make comfort feel like loyalty, that circle is a liability. You do not have to cut everyone off dramatically. But you do have to be intentional about who gets access to your time and energy, because both of those are limited and both of them are shaped by proximity.

None of these steps are complicated. They are just uncomfortable, and discomfort is exactly where the gap lives. Closing it is not a one-time decision. It is a daily one, made in small moments that nobody is watching, that stack up over time into a life that looks nothing like where you started.

That is the whole game. Decide, execute, and do not stop doing it when it gets hard, because it will get hard. That is not a warning. That is the point.

—Joseph Grimes

PART TWO

The 700 Credit Score Blueprint

Stop Playing Their Game. Start Winning.

"I am not a financial advisor. I am a guy who is extremely intentional with cash. The banks are designed to keep you poor. You need a 700+ score to stop wasting money on high interest so you can use that cash to actually get rich."

The first time I really understood what a credit score cost you, I was not sitting in a finance class. I was watching someone I knew get turned down for an apartment. Good job, steady income, never missed a day of work. And the number on a report nobody had ever taught him to manage was the reason he could not get a key. That moment stuck with me, because it was so clean and so brutal. A number you did not know existed was making decisions about your life without your input.

I grew up in a household where credit was not discussed in any useful way. What I heard was either silence or fear: people treating debt like something shameful instead of something to be understood and used strategically. Nobody explained the difference between the kind of debt that builds something and the kind that drains you. Nobody explained that your credit score is not just a financial metric, it is a tax. Every month, depending on which side of 700 you sit on, you are either being rewarded or penalized in ways that compound over decades.

I decided to learn the system the way I learned everything else: by going directly at it, understanding how it worked, and then using that understanding to my advantage. By the time I was in my twenties, I had an 800-plus score, and it opened doors. Those doors had nothing to do with my ability to take on debt and everything to do with what lenders, landlords, and partners were willing to offer someone they considered trustworthy based on a three-digit number.

This section is not about gaming the system. It is about understanding the rules of a game you are already playing whether you know it or not. The banks understand these rules completely. The question is whether you do.

CHAPTER 2.1

Know the Score

You cannot fix something you do not understand, and most people do not actually understand how their credit score is calculated. They know it exists. They know it is important. They check it occasionally, wince, and move on. That is not a strategy.

Your credit score is maintained by three reporting bureaus: Equifax, Experian, and TransUnion. They operate independently, which means the information on each report can be different, and errors on one will not automatically be corrected on the others. You need to treat all three as separate reports and check all three regularly, because a creditor pulling your report for a loan or an apartment might only check one of them.

The score itself, your FICO score, is built from five factors, and the weight of each one tells you exactly where to focus your energy.

35% Payment History. Did you pay on time? This is the biggest single factor. One missed payment can drop your score significantly and stay on your report for seven years.

30% Amount Owed. How much of your available credit are you using? This is your utilization rate, and it matters more than most people realize.

15% Length of History. How long have your accounts been open? Older accounts with clean history are worth protecting.

10% New Credit. Every time you apply for something new, it triggers a hard inquiry that temporarily lowers your score.

10% Credit Mix. Having different types of credit, like cards, installment loans, and auto, shows lenders you can manage more than one kind of debt.

The tools to check your score are free and there is no excuse not to be using them. CreditKarma.com gives you your TransUnion and Equifax scores updated weekly. Experian.com offers a free account with your Experian score. AnnualCreditReport.com is the government-authorized site where you can pull your full credit reports from all three bureaus, and most major banking apps, Chase, Bank of America, Navy Federal, now show your score directly on the dashboard.

Check your score. Check your reports. Know what is on them. You cannot dispute what you have not read.

CHAPTER 2.2

The Three Golden Rules

Everything else in this section builds on top of these three rules. If you do nothing else, do these.

Rule 1: The Phantom Limit

Your credit limit is not your spending limit. If the bank gives you a one-thousand-dollar limit, the real number you should be working with is one hundred dollars. That is not arbitrary. It comes directly from how utilization is calculated and weighted in your score.

Utilization is the ratio of what you owe to what you have available. At thirty percent utilization, your score starts to take a hit. At fifty percent, it takes a bigger one. At eighty or ninety percent, you are actively damaging your score every single month. The sweet spot is under ten percent, and the actual goal is zero, meaning you pay the balance in full before the statement closes.

Most people think the due date is what matters. It is not. The statement date is what matters. That is the date your balance gets reported to the bureaus. If you pay your balance down to zero three days before the statement date, the bureaus see a zero balance and your utilization looks perfect. If you wait until the due date, the balance has already been reported. Pay early. Pay in full. Do not carry a balance you are paying interest on when the only thing it buys you is a lower score.

Rule 2: The Power of One

You do not need a wallet full of cards. More cards do not mean a better score. They mean more accounts to manage, more opportunities to make a mistake, and more temptation to spend money you should be moving toward an asset. One card, worked correctly, can get you to an excellent score. Three is the absolute ceiling, and even that is only warranted once your financial habits are locked in.

The play with a single card is to request a credit limit increase once a year. Do this without opening new accounts and you increase your available credit, lower your utilization automatically, and build a longer relationship with one lender who gets to watch you be responsible with their money over time. That is exactly the behavior that gets rewarded.

Rule 3: Auto-Pay Everything

Payment history is thirty-five percent of your score and it is completely within your control. There is no reason to ever miss a payment in the current era of automatic payments. Set every account to auto-pay the full statement balance, not the minimum, the full balance, and the single largest factor in your credit score becomes something you never have to think about again.

The minimum payment is a trap. It keeps the account current on paper while the interest accumulates in the background and the balance barely moves. The bank loves the minimum payment. You should not.

CHAPTER 2.3

The Ghost

This is for anyone starting from zero, no score, no history, a blank file that lenders look at and decide means too much risk to touch. The problem with having no credit is that you cannot get credit without having credit, which is one of the more perfectly designed catch-22s in the financial system. Here is how you break it.

Step one is a secured credit card. Discover and Capital One both offer them and they are straightforward. You give the bank a deposit, usually around two hundred dollars, and that deposit becomes your credit limit. You are borrowing your own money, but the account reports to the bureaus like any other credit card, and that reporting is what you are after.

Once you have the card, do not carry it in your wallet. Put it in a drawer. Link it to one small monthly subscription you are already paying, a streaming service, a phone bill, whatever is fixed and predictable, and set it to auto-pay in full from your checking account. The card charges a small amount every month. The auto-pay clears it every month. You never think about it. You never touch it. And in six months you have a credit history and a score in the 680 range built entirely on autopilot.

At that point you apply for a regular unsecured card, get your deposit back, and you are in the system with a clean file and a score that gives you options. Six months of discipline for decades of access. That is the trade.

If you are a parent reading this, open a secured card for your teenager and make them an authorized user on one of your older accounts. Let the history transfer to them before they ever need to build it on their own. That is the kind of financial head start that changes a life trajectory, and it costs you nothing but the effort to set it up.

CHAPTER 2.4

The Fixer

This is for the person sitting somewhere between 580 and 680. Decent enough to be approved for things occasionally, bad enough to be paying for it in interest rates and terms that would make a reasonable person angry. You got here through a combination of missed payments, high balances, maybe a collection or two, and possibly some errors you have never bothered to dispute. All of it is fixable. None of it requires a credit repair company charging you a monthly fee to do things you can do yourself for free.

Step 1: The Authorized User Hack

Find someone in your family or close circle who has a credit card they have had for at least ten years with a perfect payment history and a score above 750. Ask them to add you as an authorized user on that account. Tell them to shred the card when it arrives. You do not need access to it and they do not need to give it to you. What you need is the account to appear on your credit report.

When it does, their ten years of perfect history copies onto your report. Their utilization on that card becomes part of your profile. Their length of history adds to yours. This is completely legal, it is how the system works, and it can move your score thirty to fifty points in thirty days without you doing anything else. It is the fastest legitimate move available to someone trying to close the gap quickly.

Step 2: Attack the Balances

If you have cards that are sitting at high utilization, meaning you owe close to the limit, your score is taking a hit every single month those balances stay high. The math is straightforward: a one-thousand-dollar limit with nine hundred dollars owed is ninety percent utilization, and ninety percent utilization is a drag on your score that no other strategy can fully offset while it is active.

Pay the highest utilization cards down first. If you cannot get to zero, get below thirty percent on every card. If you cannot do that, stop using the cards completely and let the minimum payments chip away at the balance while you redirect every available dollar toward bringing those ratios down. This is not sexy but it works, and it works faster than most people expect once the utilization numbers start to drop.

Step 3: Dispute the Errors

Pull your full reports from AnnualCreditReport.com and read every line. You are looking for anything inaccurate: wrong addresses, accounts that are not yours, balances that are incorrect, late payments marked on accounts you paid on time, accounts that should have aged off by now but have not. Errors on credit reports are more common than people realize, and the bureaus are required by law to investigate any dispute you file and correct or delete anything they cannot verify as accurate.

Disputing is free and you can do it directly on each bureau's website or by certified mail. You do not need to pay anyone to do this for you. The process takes thirty days and the results can be significant. That is especially true if you have old collections or incorrect derogatory marks sitting on your report, dragging your score down for something that either never happened or has already been resolved.

CHAPTER 2.5

The Flex

If you are at 700 or above, your credit is functional. You are getting approved, you are getting reasonable rates, and the score is doing its job. Getting from 700 to 800 is less about urgency and more about discipline over time, because at this level most of the heavy lifting is already done and what is left is patience.

The limit increase request is your primary tool here. Call each of your credit card issuers once a year and ask for a credit limit increase. Ask specifically whether they can do it without a hard inquiry. Many will. If your limit doubles and your spending stays the same, your utilization drops automatically without you changing anything about your behavior. This is the easiest point-per-effort ratio available at this stage.

After that, the strategy is to stop applying for things. Every hard inquiry from a new application temporarily lowers your score, and to get into the 800 range you want no more than one inquiry in the last twelve months. What you are really doing at this level is letting time do the work: letting your accounts get older, letting your history get cleaner, letting the score climb without interference. Discipline here looks like doing less, not more.

You do not need 800-plus to build wealth. You need 700 to access the tools that matter: good mortgage rates, business credit, competitive loan terms. Anything above that is a margin of comfort, not a requirement. Chase the 700 with urgency. Let the 800 come with time.

CHAPTER 2.6

The Safe Starter Pack

Stop letting retail stores talk you into store cards at checkout. The Gap card, the Macy's card, the credit card attached to a store you shop at twice a year. These are high-interest, low-limit products that do very little for your score and a lot for the retailer's revenue. Stay away from them.

If you want to build a strategic card setup, here is the framework based on income level and what each card is designed to do.

Card Role	Recommended Card	Rule
The Gas Card	Shell, Wawa, or local station card	Leave it in the car. Gas only.
The Grocery Card	Sam's Club Mastercard or Costco Visa	Food and household supplies only.
The Bill Payer	Discover It Secured or Amex Blue Cash	Cell phone and internet on auto-pay.

The income-to-limit targets below keep you from overextending. Your goal is not more cards. It is higher limits on fewer cards, which lowers your utilization automatically and simplifies your financial life.

Income Range	Ideal Cards	Target Total Limit
\$30k – \$45k	1 to 2 cards	\$5,000 total
\$45k – \$70k	2 to 3 cards	\$10,000 – \$15,000
\$70k – \$100k	3 cards max	\$25,000+
\$100k+	3 cards max	\$50,000+

The golden rule that sits above all of this: never carry a balance you cannot pay in full. Credit is a tool. Tools are useful when you control them and dangerous when they control you.

CHAPTER 2.7

The Templates

These are copy-and-paste scripts for two of the most powerful moves available to someone cleaning up their credit. Use them exactly as written and do not deviate. The specific language matters.

Template 1: The Pay for Delete Script

Use this when you have a balance in collections and you have the cash to settle it. The goal is not just to pay it. It is to get it removed from your report entirely in exchange for payment. Not all collectors will agree to this, but enough will that it is always worth asking before you send a dollar.

> "I am calling regarding account number [XXXX]. I am willing to settle this debt in full for [Dollar Amount] today, but only if you agree in writing to delete this trade line from my credit report entirely upon receipt of payment. I will not pay anything until I receive that agreement via email or certified letter. If you are not able to offer a pay-for-delete, I will not be making a payment at this time."

Say it and then stop talking. The silence is part of the negotiation. Get the agreement in writing before any money moves. A verbal promise from a collections agent is worth nothing.

Template 2: The Dispute Letter

Use this to dispute inaccurate information on your report. Send it by certified mail with return receipt so you have proof of delivery and a paper trail.

> To: [Bureau Name — Equifax / Experian / TransUnion]
>
> I am writing to dispute inaccurate information on my credit report. The account listed as [Account Name] with account number [XXXX] contains an error. The [balance / date / payment status] reported is incorrect.
>
> Under the Fair Credit Reporting Act, I am requesting that you investigate this item and correct or delete it from my report if it cannot be verified as fully accurate.
>
> Signed, [Your Full Name] [Your Address] [Date]

The FCRA gives the bureau thirty days to investigate. If they cannot verify the item as one hundred percent accurate, they are required to remove it. Follow up after thirty days if you do not hear back, and keep copies of everything you send.

— Joseph Grimes

PART THREE

Financial Literacy Simplified

5 Rules to Escape the Trap and Build Real Wealth

"School didn't teach you this. Your job won't teach you this. I will."

I bought my first house at twenty-four years old. I did not have a pile of cash sitting in savings. What I had was a credit score I had worked to build, a down payment I had scraped together through discipline and side income, and enough knowledge about how the process worked to not get eaten alive by it. The people who handled my closing were professional and polite, and not one of them volunteered a single piece of information I had not specifically asked for first.

That experience taught me something I have never forgotten: the financial system is not designed to educate you. It is designed to process you. The mortgage broker gets paid when you close. The car dealership gets paid when you sign. The credit card company gets paid every month you carry a balance. The system runs on your lack of knowledge, and the less you understand about how it works, the more profitable you are to everyone operating inside it.

I grew up in Orlando and nobody at my dinner table talked about assets, cash flow, tax strategy, or the difference between good debt and the kind that keeps you broke for a decade. We talked about survival. And the transition from survival thinking to wealth-building thinking is not automatic. It requires someone to sit down and explain the rules of a game most people do not even know they are playing.

This section is that conversation. Five rules that separate the people building something real from the people who work their entire lives and end up with nothing to show for it. Just a pension they can barely live on and a house that the bank technically owns for another twelve years.

CHAPTER 3.1

The Trap

Most people are running a race they cannot win, and the cruelest part is that the race was designed to look winnable from the starting line.

You go to school because that is what you are supposed to do. You get a degree, take on debt to pay for it, and enter the workforce carrying a balance you will spend the next decade paying off. You get a job, and the job comes with a paycheck, and the paycheck feels like progress until you realize the government has already taken their share before the money ever reaches your account. You buy a car to get to the job, and the car needs insurance and maintenance and eventually a replacement, so you finance another one. You buy a house because everyone tells you it is an asset and renting is throwing money away. Then you spend thirty years paying a mortgage, property taxes, insurance, and repairs on a property you do not actually own yet.

At the end of all of it, forty years of work, forty years of showing up, you have a 401k that the market can cut in half on a bad year, a house that might be paid off, and a monthly Social Security check that was never designed to actually replace your income. That is the trap. It is not dramatic. It does not announce itself. It just absorbs your entire working life in exchange for the appearance of stability.

The wealthy play a completely different game. They do not work for money. They deploy money to generate more money, and then they use the tax code to keep as much of it as possible. They are not smarter than you. They are playing by a different set of rules, and those rules have been available the entire time. Nobody is coming to explain them to you. That is what this section is for.

CHAPTER 3.2

Rule 1 — Assets vs. Liabilities

"An asset puts money in your pocket every month. A liability takes money out. Everything else is just vocabulary."

Forget the accounting textbook definition. The version that actually matters for building wealth is simpler than that, and once you internalize it, you will never look at a purchase the same way again.

An asset puts money into your pocket every month. A liability takes money out. That is the whole framework. Everything you own falls into one of those two categories, and most people's financial lives are dominated by the second one while they convince themselves they are building something.

The House Lie

The most widespread financial myth in America is that your primary residence is an asset. People repeat this constantly, and it is almost always wrong. If you live in your house, you pay a mortgage every month, property taxes every year, insurance every year, and maintenance whenever something breaks. Money is leaving your pocket. By the definition that actually matters, that house is a liability.

It becomes an asset the moment someone else is paying you to live in it, when the rent covers the mortgage plus expenses and generates positive cash flow on top. That version of a house is an asset. The version you are living in while making payments is not, and calling it one does not make it one.

This does not mean you should not own a home. It means you should be honest about what it is in your financial picture so you are not counting it as wealth when it is actually an expense.

The Car Lie

Unless you are generating income with your vehicle through rideshare, delivery, or turo rentals, your car is a liability. It loses value the moment you drive it off the lot, costs you in insurance and maintenance every month, and is financed at an interest rate that means you are paying significantly more than the sticker price by the time it is yours. The car does not care how good it makes you look. It cares about the monthly payment it extracts from your account.

The wealthy buy cars differently. They drive reliable paid-off vehicles until their assets generate enough monthly cash flow to absorb a car payment without touching their liquidity. Then they buy the car they want from a position of strength, not because they stretched their budget and signed a note. There is a version of that car in your future. Just make sure it comes after the assets, not before.

What You Should Actually Be Buying

Liabilities (Stop Buying These)	**Assets (Start Buying These)**
New cars on five-year notes	Rental properties with positive cash flow
Designer clothes and shoes	Dividend-paying stocks and index funds
Jewelry and luxury goods	Businesses that generate monthly revenue
Boats and recreational vehicles	Equipment that generates income
Timeshares	Short-term rental properties

The goal is not to deprive yourself forever. The goal is to build the assets first so that the assets pay for the lifestyle, instead of the lifestyle consuming everything before the assets ever get built.

CHAPTER 3.3

Rule 2 — Cash Flow is King

"Net worth is vanity. Cash flow is sanity. You can be a millionaire on paper and still be broke on a Tuesday."

Net worth is a snapshot. It tells you what your assets would be worth if you liquidated everything today and paid off everything you owe. It is a useful number for certain things and a deeply misleading one for others. A person can have a net worth of two million dollars, mostly tied up in a home and a retirement account they cannot touch for twenty years. They still might not be able to cover an unexpected four-thousand-dollar expense without going into debt. That is not wealth.

That is an illusion of wealth with a very nice number attached to it.

Cash flow is what actually runs your life. It is the money that hits your account every month after all your expenses are covered. Positive cash flow means you have more coming in than going out. Negative cash flow means you are slowly going underwater no matter what your net worth says. The wealthy obsess over cash flow because they understand that cash flow is what buys your freedom, not the number on a statement you look at once a quarter.

The Formula

Income minus expenses equals cash flow. If your income is four thousand a month and your expenses are thirty-eight hundred, your cash flow is two hundred dollars. That two hundred is your margin, your investment capital, and your safety net all at once. It is also not enough, which means your only two options are to increase income or decrease expenses, and decreasing expenses has a floor. You can only cut so far before you are cutting into your quality of life in ways that are not sustainable.

Increasing income has no ceiling. That is why the strategy is always to build additional income streams rather than to optimize your way to freedom on a single paycheck. A side business, a rental unit, freelance income, dividends: any one of these that generates consistent monthly cash adds to your margin and moves you closer to the point where your passive income covers your expenses. That is the day you are financially free, and it has nothing to do with your net worth and everything to do with your monthly cash flow math.

Active vs. Passive Income

Active income is what you trade time for. Your salary. Your hourly rate. Your freelance project. The moment you stop working, the income stops. This is where everyone starts, and there is nothing wrong with it. But it cannot be where you stay, because time is finite and you will eventually run out of it.

Passive income is what your assets generate while you sleep. Rent from a property. Dividends from stocks. Revenue from a business that runs without you. The goal is to build enough passive income that it exceeds your expenses, at which point work becomes optional. Not because you stop working. Most people who achieve this keep working because they want to. It is that you are no longer working out of necessity. That distinction changes everything about how you show up in every area of your life.

CHAPTER 3.4

Rule 3 — Credit as a Tool

"The middle class uses credit to buy toys. The wealthy use credit to buy assets. Same tool, completely different outcome."

Part Two of this book covered how to build and protect your credit score in detail, so this chapter is not about the mechanics. It is about the mindset. Because the difference between someone who uses credit well and someone who gets destroyed by it is not knowledge of the system. It is their relationship with what the system is for.

For most people, a high credit score is a badge that unlocks bigger purchases. A better car. A nicer apartment. A credit card with a higher limit that makes it easier to spend money they do not have on things they do not need. This is using credit as a consumption tool, and consumption tools do not build wealth. They transfer it, from your account to someone else's.

For the person playing the long game, a high credit score is access to borrowed money, and borrowed money is how you speed up asset acquisition without waiting until you have enough cash saved to buy things outright. Borrowing at six percent to buy a rental property that generates twelve percent returns is not debt, it is an arbitrage. You are using the bank's money to generate returns that exceed the cost of borrowing it. That is a completely different transaction than borrowing at twenty percent to buy a television.

Good Debt vs. Bad Debt

Bad Debt	**Good Debt**
Borrowing at 20% to buy a TV	Borrowing at 6% to buy a rental property
Car loan on a depreciating vehicle	Business loan to buy income-generating equipment
Credit card balance carried month to month	Mortgage on a cash-flowing investment property
Buy now, pay later on consumer goods	SBA loan to launch or expand a business

The ultimate goal is cash. When you own something outright, no mortgage, no lien, no note, no one can take it from you regardless of what the economy does. In the beginning you likely do not have the cash, which is why you build the credit. Once the credit gets you into the asset, the asset generates the cash flow that eventually pays off the credit and leaves you holding something free and clear. That is the sequence. Credit to access. Assets to generate. Cash flow to own.

CHAPTER 3.5

Rule 4 — Sweat Equity

"You cannot save your way to financial freedom. You have to build your way there, and building starts with whatever you have right now."

If you are reading this making fifteen, eighteen, twenty dollars an hour, I need you to hear this clearly: the path to financial freedom is not about waiting until you have enough money to start investing. If you wait for that moment, it will never come, because the expenses in your life will expand to consume whatever income you generate and you will always be six months away from being ready.

The path is sweat equity. It is trading your time and your energy for assets when you cannot yet trade your cash for them. It is painting the walls of your first rental property yourself instead of hiring a contractor, because the two thousand dollars you save on labor becomes part of the equity you are building. It is working the night shift at the job and spending your days building the business. It is saying no to things that feel good in the short term because you can see clearly where the money needs to go instead.

I painted walls. I mowed lawns. I drove to job sites and managed contractors on weekends while working full time during the week. That was what phase one required, and I understood that phase one does not last forever if you do not treat it like it does. The people who stay stuck in phase one are the ones who refuse to do it with urgency. They treat the hustle like a lifestyle instead of a temporary condition, and temporary conditions only become permanent when you stop pushing through them.

Phase One: The Grind

You work the job. You come home and work the side hustle or the business. Every dollar that is not a necessity goes toward one thing: acquiring your first asset. Not the vacation. Not the upgrade. The asset. This phase is supposed to be uncomfortable. That discomfort is the price of everything that comes after it.

A Word About the Stock Market

Putting fifty dollars a month into a brokerage account is not a strategy for freedom, it is a strategy for eventually having something at sixty-five that the market can cut in half before you get to spend it. Index funds and dividend stocks matter later in the journey, when you have cash flow to deploy at scale. In phase one, they are a distraction that makes people feel like they are investing. Really they are just delaying the harder work of building something that generates real returns on a timeline that actually matters to their life.

Build the first asset with sweat. Use the cash flow from that asset to buy the second one without as much sweat. Use the cash flow from both to start building the portfolio. That is the sequence, and the sequence only starts when you put your body into it before your bank account is ready.

CHAPTER 3.6

Rule 5 — The Tax Cheat Code

"There are two sets of tax rules in America. One for employees. One for business owners. Nobody tells you this at orientation."

The way taxes work for an employee is straightforward and brutal. You earn money, the government takes their share off the top before the money ever reaches you, and you live on whatever is left. You are taxed on your gross income, and the only deductions available to you are a handful of things like mortgage interest and student loan payments that barely move the needle.

The way taxes work for a business owner is a completely different system operating under the same tax code. You earn revenue, you spend money on legitimate business expenses, and you pay taxes on what is left after those expenses. You are taxed on the net, not the gross, and the gap between those two numbers can be significant when you understand what qualifies as a business expense.

Your cell phone, if you use it for business, is a business expense. The portion of your home used as a dedicated office is a business expense. Your vehicle mileage driven for business purposes is a business expense. The meals you have with clients and business associates are partially deductible. The courses, books, and conferences related to your industry are business expenses. The government has built these deductions into the tax code deliberately, because small business owners create jobs and economic activity, and the code rewards that. The problem is that nobody explains this to you when you are an employee, because when you are an employee, none of it applies.

Forming an LLC does not require a lawyer or a complicated process. Part Four of this book walks you through exactly how to do it. Once it is done, you have access to the second set of rules, and the second set of rules changes your relationship with money permanently.

What This Looks Like in Practice

Employee Tax Reality	**Business Owner Tax Reality**
Taxed on gross income	Taxed on net income after expenses
No deduction for cell phone	Cell phone is a deductible business expense
No deduction for vehicle use	Business mileage is deductible
No deduction for home office	Dedicated home office space is deductible
Limited deductions available	Business meals, travel, education all deductible

This is not a loophole. It is the tax code working exactly as designed. The question is not whether these advantages exist. They do, and the wealthy have been using them legally for generations. The question is whether you are positioned to access them. An LLC is a one-time filing that costs between fifty and three hundred dollars depending on your state. The tax savings over a lifetime of business ownership dwarf that number before the first year is out.

CHAPTER 3.7

The Infinite Banking Move

"Buy. Borrow. Die. That is the billionaire playbook, and it is completely legal."

This is the part of the financial system that most people never learn about because it only becomes relevant once you have assets, and most people never build assets. But I want you to understand this now, before you have the assets, because understanding where you are going changes how you build toward it.

Billionaires and ultra-high-net-worth individuals have a problem that sounds absurd to most people: they own enormous amounts of wealth in assets like real estate, stocks, and business equity. But if they sell those assets to access the cash, they trigger a capital gains tax event that can cost them twenty, thirty percent or more of the value. So they do not sell. They borrow.

They go to a bank and say they have ten million dollars in real estate or securities, and they want a loan using those assets as collateral. The bank gives them a million dollars in cash. That cash is a loan, not income, so it is not taxable. They spend it on more assets, or on their lifestyle, and the assets they borrowed against continue to appreciate and generate cash flow that services the loan. They live like kings on borrowed money, their net worth keeps growing, and they pay a fraction of what an employee pays in taxes. They have structured their entire financial life around one principle: you pay taxes on income, and loans are not income.

The Real Estate Version

This is something I do with my own properties, and it is more accessible than most people think. You buy a property. You fix it up and force appreciation, meaning you increase the value through improvements rather than waiting for the market to do it on its own. Once the property is worth significantly more than you paid for it, you go to the bank and refinance. The bank gives you a check for the equity you have built. That check is not income, it is a loan against the property, so you do not pay taxes on it. You keep the property. You keep the tenants paying rent, which covers the new mortgage payment. And you have a pile of tax-free cash to put into the next deal.

This is the engine. Buy, improve, refinance, repeat. Each cycle pulls equity out of existing assets and deploys it into new ones without triggering a tax event. Over time the portfolio grows, the cash flow compounds, and the distance between your financial position and where you started becomes hard to explain to people who never learned that this was possible.

You do not start with ten million dollars in real estate. You start with one property and one refinance and a willingness to understand the system well enough to use it. The principle scales from a single rental unit all the way to a portfolio that generates more monthly income than most people make in a year.

CHAPTER 3.8

The Blueprint

Everything in this section is connected, and the sequence matters as much as the individual steps. Here is the path from where you are to where this is all pointing.

Phase 1: Stabilization

Get your credit score above 700. Stop acquiring liabilities you cannot afford. Build your emergency fund to cover three months of expenses. Maximize your active income through your job, side hustle, or both. This phase is about creating stability and margin. You cannot invest what you do not have.

Phase 2: Acquisition

Use your credit and your saved capital to acquire your first cash-flowing asset. A rental property, a small business, a piece of equipment that generates revenue: something that produces income you did not have to trade an hour of your time to create. Do not put your money in a savings account earning a fraction of a percent. Buy something that works for you.

Phase 3: Optimization

Form your LLC if you have not already. Run your legitimate business expenses through it to reduce your taxable income. Reinvest every dollar of profit from your assets into the next asset. Request refinances on properties that have appreciated. Stack the cash flow.

Phase 4: Liberation

Your passive income now exceeds your monthly expenses. Work becomes a choice. You use the buy-borrow strategy to access equity in your assets without selling them and without creating tax events. Your portfolio generates enough cash flow to fund your lifestyle and continue growing simultaneously. You are free.

None of these phases happen by accident. They happen because someone decided to understand the system well enough to use it, and then did the work in the right order with enough patience to let it compound. The timeline looks different for everyone. The sequence does not.

You now have the rules. The question is whether you are going to use them or file them away with everything else you know you should do and never quite got around to.

— Joseph Grimes

PART FOUR

The 10-Step Business Launchpad

Stop Talking About It. Be About It.

"Gatekeeping ends today. Here is the paperwork, the plan, and the truth about getting rich."

Every year, millions of people say they want to start a business. They talk about it at barbecues and post about it on social media and tell people close to them that it is coming soon, and then the year ends and nothing is different except the date. I know because I was in that orbit for a while before I stopped talking and started filing.

The gap between wanting to own a business and actually owning one is mostly paperwork and nerve. Not capital. Not connections. Not timing. Paperwork and nerve. The paperwork is what this section covers in full detail, and the nerve is something you are going to have to bring yourself, because nobody can hand you that.

What I have watched over and over again is people overcomplicating the start. They spend months researching LLCs and business plans and funding options and logos, and they mistake that research for progress because it feels productive. It is not progress. Progress is a filed document. Progress is an open bank account. Progress is a first customer paying you money for a thing you built. Everything else is delay with better vocabulary.

I built three businesses. None of them started with a perfect plan. All of them started with a decision and a filing. This section gives you the ten steps in the exact order they need to happen so that when you close this book, you have no excuse left that a Google search and thirty minutes cannot eliminate.

CHAPTER 4.1

The Wake-Up Call

The statistics on business ownership in this country are not inspiring, and I am going to put them in front of you anyway because comfortable people do not build things. Uncomfortable people do.

2.4% of employer businesses in the United States are owned by Black Americans, despite representing 14.4% of the population.

8x the wealth gap between the average white family and the average Black family.

20% of new businesses fail in the first year. 50% are gone by year five.

Those numbers are not destiny. They are a scoreboard, and scoreboards exist to be changed. The reason the gap persists is not talent and it is not work ethic. It is access to capital, access to knowledge, and access to the blueprint that people in business-building families absorb before they ever start their first company. That blueprint is what this section is.

We are consumers by habit and owners by choice, and the choice is available right now. The barriers to starting a legitimate business in this country are lower than they have ever been. You can form an LLC for fifty dollars, open a business bank account online in twenty minutes, build a website for free, and reach your first customers through social media without spending a dollar on advertising. The tools are there. The question is whether you are going to pick them up.

CHAPTER 4.2

Step 1 — The EIN

"Stop paying people $300 to do something that is free."

The EIN, the Employer Identification Number, is your business's version of a Social Security Number. It is what identifies your business to the federal government, what you need to open a business bank account, what you put on contracts and invoices, and what separates you legally from operating as just a person with a hobby. You need this before you need almost anything else.

Here is the scam: if you Google 'get an EIN,' the first three or four results are paid services charging anywhere from fifty to three hundred dollars to file this on your behalf. Do not click them. The IRS issues EINs directly, it takes about ten minutes, and it costs nothing.

How to Get Your EIN Right Now

Go to IRS.gov. Use the search bar and type 'Apply for EIN Online.' Click the link that takes you to the official IRS application. Answer the questions about your business structure. If you are a single-member LLC or a sole proprietor just starting out, the process is straightforward. Submit the form and the IRS generates your EIN as a PDF immediately. Download it, save it in at least three places, and do not lose it.

Without this number you are not a business. You are a person doing things informally, and informally is the most expensive way to operate because you have no legal protection, no ability to open a proper business account, no foundation for building business credit, and no credibility with vendors, partners, or clients who ask for it. Get the EIN today. It takes less time than watching a YouTube video about getting an EIN.

CHAPTER 4.3

Step 2 — The LLC

The EIN registers you with the federal government. The LLC registers you with your state. You need both, and they serve different purposes.

An LLC, a Limited Liability Company, is the legal structure that separates you as a person from your business as an entity. This distinction is not bureaucratic. It is the difference between a lawsuit against your business being able to reach your personal bank account, your car, and your home versus being limited to what the business itself holds. Without an LLC, you and your business are legally the same thing. Someone who sues your business sues you personally. That exposure is real and it has ended people financially who thought they were protected when they were not.

The document you are filing is called the Articles of Organization, and the process is simpler than it sounds.

How to File Your Articles of Organization

Go to Google and search 'Secretary of State Business Search' followed by your state name. Every state has an online portal for business filings. Before you file, do a name search to confirm your chosen business name is not already taken by another registered entity in your state. Once the name is clear, find the link for filing Articles of Organization and complete the form. The cost varies by state. Some states charge as little as fifty dollars, others charge up to three hundred. This is one of the only costs in this process you cannot avoid, and it is worth every dollar.

Once your LLC is filed and approved, keep your approval documents with your EIN. These two documents together are what you bring to a bank to open a business account, what you show clients who ask for proof of your business structure, and what establishes your legal existence as an operating entity rather than a side operation someone can dismiss.

One important note: if you are running any kind of business right now without an LLC and something goes wrong, whether a client dispute, an accident, or a liability claim, everything you own personally is on the table. File the LLC. Protect your family before you need to, not after.

CHAPTER 4.4

Step 3 — The Licenses

Having an LLC means you legally exist. It does not mean you are legally allowed to operate in every context. Depending on your industry, your city, and the type of work you are doing, you may need additional permissions before you can operate without risk.

This is the step most new business owners skip because it feels like more bureaucracy after they just spent time on the EIN and the LLC. But operating without the required licenses exposes you to fines, forced closure, and in some industries, personal liability that your LLC cannot shield you from.

Sales Tax License

If you are selling physical products, whether clothing, food, or goods of any kind, your state requires you to collect sales tax from customers and remit it to the Department of Revenue. This requires a Sales Tax ID or Sales Tax Permit, which you register for through your state's Department of Revenue website. The registration is typically free. Operating without it and collecting sales tax you are not remitting, or failing to collect it when you should, is a compliance issue that compounds quickly.

Local Permits

If you are opening a physical location, whether a barbershop, a food truck, a salon, or a retail space, your city or county has requirements that your state filing does not cover. Zoning permits, health department inspections, fire safety compliance, signage permits: all of these are local and all of them are separate from your state LLC filing. Call your City Hall or visit the county clerk's website and ask directly: 'I am starting a [type of business]. What permits do I need to operate legally?' They will tell you. This call takes fifteen minutes and saves you from being shut down after you have already invested money in the space.

Professional Licenses

Some industries are regulated at the state level and require a specific license before you can legally charge for your services. Cosmetology, barbering, real estate, financial advising, contracting, trucking, childcare: all of these have licensing requirements that vary by state and that your LLC does not satisfy on its own. If your business is in one of these categories, research the specific licensing body for your profession in your state and understand the requirements before you start taking clients. Operating without a required professional license is not just a business risk. In some cases it is a criminal one.

CHAPTER 4.5

Step 4 — The Bank Account

"Co-mingling your personal and business money is the single fastest way to destroy everything you just built."

This is the step that separates people who are serious about their business from people who are playing at it. Co-mingling, mixing your personal money with your business money in the same account, is one of the most common and most damaging mistakes new business owners make, and it happens for one reason: it feels easier in the short term.

The cost of that convenience is enormous. First, it destroys your liability protection. One of the primary reasons you formed an LLC was to create a legal separation between you and your business. When you mix your money, courts can argue that separation never actually existed, a concept called 'piercing the corporate veil,' and suddenly your personal assets are exposed to claims against the business. Second, it makes tax time a nightmare. When your business revenue and your grocery runs are in the same account, separating legitimate business expenses from personal ones becomes a months-long exercise in frustration. It either costs you a lot of money in accounting fees or costs you in missed deductions you could not document cleanly. Third, it makes it impossible to know whether your business is actually profitable, because you cannot see the business's financial picture clearly when it is mixed in with your personal life.

How to Open the Account

Take your EIN and your Articles of Organization to a bank. Business-friendly options include Navy Federal Credit Union, Chase Business, Bank of America Business, and online options like Relay and Mercury, which are particularly good for new businesses because they have low or no fees and clean interfaces built for tracking cash flow. Tell them you want to open a business checking account. They will handle the rest.

Once the account is open, every dollar your business earns goes into it. Every business expense comes out of it. When you need to pay yourself, you transfer money from the business account to your personal account as an owner's draw. That transfer is documented, clean, and defensible. Everything else stays separate, always.

CHAPTER 4.6

Step 5 — Funding and Credit

Most businesses do not need as much startup capital as people think, and most people use the absence of capital as a reason not to start when they could be starting with what they have and building toward what they need. Part Five of this book is entirely dedicated to businesses you can launch for under four hundred dollars, so if capital is your current obstacle, that section solves it.

But if you are building something that requires equipment, inventory, a vehicle, or a physical space, you are going to need access to money that is not sitting in your personal savings, and the SBA is where most small business owners find it.

What the SBA Actually Is

The Small Business Administration does not lend you money directly. What it does is guarantee a portion of the loan on your behalf, which reduces the risk for the bank and makes lenders far more willing to extend capital to businesses that would otherwise be considered too risky. SBA-backed loans typically come with lower interest rates, longer repayment terms, and more favorable conditions than conventional business loans. But they come with requirements that you need to be prepared for.

You generally need a credit score of 680 or above, which is why Part Two of this book comes before this one. You need a business plan that demonstrates you understand your market, your competition, your revenue model, and your path to profitability. You need at least some operating history in many cases, which is another reason to start now even if you start small. Every month of documented revenue is evidence that your business is real.

Business Credit

Separate from your personal credit, your business can build its own credit profile over time. It starts with your EIN and your business bank account. It grows through consistent on-time payments on business accounts, vendor relationships that report to business credit bureaus, and a Dun and Bradstreet DUNS number, which you can register for free at DNB.com. Business credit takes time to build, but once it exists it allows you to access capital based on the business's financial history rather than your personal score, which protects your personal credit and scales your borrowing capacity significantly.

Grants

Grants exist and some of them are specifically designed for minority-owned, women-owned, or veteran-owned small businesses. Grants.gov is the federal database, and your local Small Business Development Center, which you can find through SBA.gov, will know about state and local grant programs that are not widely advertised. The application process for grants is competitive and time-consuming, and you should pursue them in parallel with building your business rather than waiting on them as a prerequisite to starting. Build the business. Apply for the grants. Do not make one contingent on the other.

CHAPTER 4.7

Step 6 — The Skill Stack

You have the paperwork. You have the bank account. You might even have funding on the way. None of that makes you a business owner yet. What makes you a business owner is the ability to actually deliver the thing you are selling and run every function of the operation until you can afford to delegate them.

Most new entrepreneurs dramatically underestimate how many roles they are walking into simultaneously. In your first year, you are the product or service provider, the salesperson, the marketer, the customer service department, the accountant, the operations manager, and the janitor. There is no corporate support structure. There is no HR department to handle a difficult situation. There is no IT person when something breaks. There is just you, and whether the business survives its first year is almost entirely a function of whether you can handle being all of those things at once without completely falling apart.

The skill you cannot outsource in the beginning is sales. If you are scared to ask people for money, if the idea of telling a stranger what you offer and what it costs makes you want to find something else to do, entrepreneurship will punish you for that. Every business lives and dies by its ability to convert interest into revenue, and in the early stages that conversion depends entirely on you. Part Six of this book covers the sale in full. Read it, apply it, and practice it until the discomfort goes away.

The second skill you cannot fake is understanding your own operation. Before you hire anyone to do any part of your business, you need to know how that part works. When you do not understand the job, employees can underperform without consequence because you have no baseline for what good looks like. When you do understand it, you set the standard, you recognize deviation from it, and you make corrections before small problems become expensive ones.

Hire slowly. Hire people who are better than you at the specific thing you are hiring for. Document everything so that the business can function without any single person, including you. And keep learning, because every stage of growth in a business requires a different version of you than the one who started it.

CHAPTER 4.8

Step 7 — Marketing

"The number one reason businesses fail is not the product. It is obscurity. Nobody knows you exist."

You can have the best product, the cleanest service, the most competitive pricing in your market, and if the right people do not know you exist, none of it matters.

Obscurity is the silent killer of businesses that could have been something, and it kills them without drama, while the owner keeps waiting for word of mouth to do the work that consistent marketing is supposed to do.

Marketing is not optional. It is the oxygen of your business. The moment you stop pumping it in, the business starts dying, and the symptoms show up in your revenue before you even recognize the cause. I have watched people treat marketing as the thing they will do more of once the business picks up, without understanding that the business does not pick up until the marketing does. You do not wait to market until you are busy. You market consistently so that you become busy.

The Shame Factor

A significant number of people who start businesses in communities like ours hold back on marketing because of shame. They are afraid people will laugh. They do not want to post on social media because it feels vulnerable and they do not want to look like they are trying too hard or, worse, failing publicly. This is one of the most expensive fears a business owner can have, and it is entirely about ego.

Let people laugh. The ones laughing are not writing you checks anyway. The ones who are going to pay you are out there right now not knowing you exist, and the only thing standing between them and becoming your customer is your willingness to show up consistently and tell them what you do. Post daily. Talk to strangers. Tell everyone in your orbit what your business does and what problem it solves. The embarrassment is temporary. The revenue is not.

The Strategy

You do not need a marketing budget to build a customer base in the early stages. You need a phone with a camera, a social media account, and the discipline to show up every single day. Before-and-after content performs across virtually every service-based industry. Short videos showing your process build trust faster than any ad. Responding to every comment and every message is customer service that doubles as marketing. And asking satisfied customers to refer one person they know costs nothing and compounds over time into a referral network that runs on its own.

As you generate revenue, put a percentage back into paid marketing. Even twenty dollars a day in targeted ads on the right platform can generate meaningful returns for a local service business. But start with consistency and authenticity before you spend a dollar. The algorithm rewards people who show up, and so do customers.

CHAPTER 4.9

Step 8 — The Discipline Gap

This is the step nobody puts in their business plan and everybody encounters in their first year. The discipline gap is the distance between what you said you would do when you were excited about the idea and what you actually do when the reality of running a business starts to feel like a second job that does not pay you yet.

When you worked for someone else, there was a structure that kept you accountable whether you liked it or not. A schedule. A manager. A clock to punch. Consequences for not showing up. Entrepreneurship removes all of that and replaces it with total freedom. And total freedom is terrifying for anyone who has not developed the internal discipline to function without external accountability.

Nobody is coming to check on you. Nobody is going to call you if you sleep until noon. Nobody is going to notice if you skip a day of marketing or let a week go by without following up with leads. The business will just get smaller while your routine stays comfortable, and six months later you will wonder why the revenue never came.

The discipline required to build a business is not the same as the discipline required to be a good employee. It is harder, because the consequences are not immediate and the rewards are not guaranteed. You can work incredibly hard for months and see very little in return before the momentum builds. Most people quit in that window because the feedback loop is too slow and the doubt is too loud. The ones who make it through that window are not the most talented or the most connected. They are the most consistent.

Build your schedule before you need it. Decide what your business hours are and treat them the way you would treat a job. Decide what your non-negotiable daily activities are, the marketing, the follow-ups, the service delivery, the administrative tasks, and do them every single day regardless of how you feel. Feelings are not a business strategy. Consistency is.

CHAPTER 4.10

Step 9 — Ten Industries Worth Your Time

If you do not know what to start, the barrier is not capital and it is not credentials. It is decision. Here are ten industries with low startup costs, high demand, and a clear path to meaningful income for anyone willing to put in the work.

1. Residential and Commercial Cleaning

Why it works: Demand is constant, startup costs are minimal, and clients tend to be recurring. One good client can anchor your schedule for months.

Startup cost: Under $300 for supplies and basic equipment.

The play: *Start with residential, build a reputation, then move into commercial contracts where the margins are higher and the volume is larger.*

2. Trucking and Hot Shot Delivery

Why it works: The supply chain needs drivers and the shortage is not going away. A CDL and a clean record can generate six figures in your first year.

Startup cost: CDL training varies by state, typically $3,000 to $7,000, often financed through the school.

The play: *Get your CDL, lease your first truck through a program, build your authority, then move toward owning your equipment outright.*

3. Mobile Car Detailing

Why it works: You go to the customer. Rich people value their time more than their money. A clean car is a non-negotiable for a lot of your target clients.

Startup cost: Under $400 for a solid starter kit.

The play: *Target office parks and professional buildings. One building with fifty cars in the lot is fifty potential customers you can reach in one trip.*

4. Vending Machines

Why it works: Passive income with low daily involvement once your route is established. The machine works while you sleep.

Startup cost: $1,500 to $3,000 for a quality used machine. Start with one location, prove the math, then expand.

The play: *Location is everything. Negotiate placement in gyms, office buildings, laundromats, and apartment complexes. The product sells itself if the foot traffic is right.*

5. Notary Public and Loan Signing Agent

Why it works: Costs almost nothing to get started, requires minimal time investment per appointment, and the real estate market keeps demand steady.

Startup cost: Under $200 for your commission and supplies.

The play: *Get certified as a Notary Signing Agent through the National Notary Association, build a profile on Snapdocs and Signing Agent platforms, and the assignments come to you.*

6. Landscaping and Lawn Care

Why it works: Grass grows every week. Demand is seasonal but predictable, and recurring clients make your schedule and your cash flow consistent.

Startup cost: Under $500 if you start with a push mower and basic tools, scaling to a trailer and commercial equipment as revenue grows.

The play: *Offer a monthly contract, not just one-time cuts. A client who pays you monthly for the season is worth ten times a one-time customer.*

7. Social Media Management

Why it works: Every business needs a social media presence and most business owners hate doing it. If you can create content, write captions, and understand engagement, you have a marketable skill.

Startup cost: Zero dollars. Your phone and your existing knowledge are the product.

The play: *Start by offering one free month to a local business you believe in. Document the results. Use those results to get the next client at a paid rate.*

8. Power Washing

Why it works: High visual satisfaction, strong word-of-mouth, and a service that sells itself. Before-and-after photos do your marketing for you.

Startup cost: A quality pressure washer runs $400 to $800. Used equipment on Facebook Marketplace can cut that in half.

The play: *One machine on a good day generates $500 or more. Target driveways, decks, commercial storefronts, and property management companies with multiple buildings.*

9. Handyman Services

Why it works: People have genuinely lost the ability to fix basic things around their homes. If you can mount a TV, patch drywall, fix a leaky faucet, or assemble furniture, you have a service people will pay for without hesitation.

Startup cost: A solid tool set runs $200 to $400.

The play: *List on TaskRabbit and Thumbtack, respond to every inquiry within minutes, and do work that makes people feel safe recommending you. Referrals run this business.*

10. Beauty Services

Why it works: Recession-proof. People will always spend money to look good regardless of what the economy is doing. Lashes, braids, barbering, and skincare all carry strong margins and deeply loyal repeat clientele.

Startup cost: Varies by specialty. Most can be started for under $500 in supplies once you have your license.

The play: *Build your book on social media before you open a physical location. Clients follow the person, not the address. Once your book is full, the location pays for itself.*

CHAPTER 4.11

Step 10 — The Free Resource List

One of the best-kept secrets about starting a business in America is how many free, high-quality resources exist specifically to help you do it. Most people never use them because nobody points them to them. Here they are.

SCORE.org

score.org

Free mentorship from retired executives and experienced business professionals. You can request a mentor in your specific industry and get one-on-one guidance on everything from your business plan to your financials. This is the resource most people sleep on and it is completely free.

SBA.gov

sba.gov

The Small Business Administration's website has guides on writing business plans, finding local resources, understanding loan programs, and managing every stage of small business ownership. Also use it to find your local Small Business Development Center, which offers free consulting and workshops.

IRS.gov — Free File and Business Resources

irs.gov

Beyond the EIN application, the IRS website has free resources on business taxes, deductions, and your obligations as a business owner. Understanding your tax responsibilities before you need them saves you from expensive surprises.

Your Public Library

Check your local branch

Most public libraries offer free access to business databases like ReferenceUSA and IBISWorld that would cost hundreds of dollars per month to access individually. These tools let you research your target market, understand industry benchmarks, and find potential customers by geography and industry. Get a library card.

Canva

canva.com

Free design tool for logos, flyers, social media content, and business presentations. The free tier is sufficient for everything a new business needs visually. No design experience required.

DNB.com — Dun and Bradstreet

dnb.com

Register your business for a free DUNS number, which is how the business credit system tracks your company. This is the foundation of your business credit profile and costs nothing to establish.

The resources exist. The knowledge is available. The steps are documented above in the exact order they need to happen. What is left is entirely on you, and that is not a criticism. It is an opportunity. Most people will read this and go back to what they were doing. The ones who act on it will be running businesses before the year is out.

File the EIN. File the LLC. Open the account. Build the skill. Show up every day. Everything else is a detail.

— Joseph Grimes

PART FIVE

The $400 Startup

10 Businesses You Can Launch This Weekend for Less Than $400

"Stop asking for a job. Create one. The blueprint to your first $100k."

Everything in this section was built for one specific person: the person who is done waiting. The person who is tired of job interviews and shift schedules and someone else deciding what their time is worth. The person who does not have a business school background or a trust fund or a mentor who went before them and mapped the path.

If that is you, then you have something more valuable than any of those things right now. You have a reason. And a strong enough reason, combined with a pressure washer or a set of hand tools or a shop vac and an extension cord, is enough to change your income before this month is over.

I wrote this for the young hustler who is tired of hearing no. I wrote it for the man re-entering society after a stretch who needs income that does not require a background check to access. I wrote it for the single parent who cannot afford to spend three years building something before it generates a dollar. Every business on this list can be started this weekend. Every one of them has a clear path to a hundred thousand dollars a year in revenue. None of them require a degree, a loan, or anyone's permission.

What they do require is that you actually start.

CHAPTER 5.1

The Framework

The $333 Rule

One hundred thousand dollars a year sounds like a big number until you break it into a daily target. Assuming you work three hundred days a year, taking Sundays and major holidays off, you need to generate three hundred and thirty-three dollars per day to hit six figures. That is the number you wake up hunting every morning. Once you hit it, your day is done. Some days you will exceed it. Some days you will fall short. But the target is clear, it is specific, and it is achievable in every single business on this list.

The power of the daily target is that it converts an intimidating annual number into a manageable daily problem. You are not trying to make a hundred thousand dollars. You are trying to make three hundred and thirty-three dollars today. That shift in framing changes everything about how you approach the work.

Sweat Equity Over Capital

Every business on this list is low cash and high effort. That is the trade at this stage, and it is a good one. The equity you are building is not financial yet. It is reputational, operational, and experiential. You are learning how to run a business, how to find and keep customers, how to price your work, how to manage your time, and how to show up consistently in conditions that are not always comfortable. Those skills are worth more than the startup capital, and they transfer to every business you will ever build after this one.

The Owner's Tax Advantage

The moment you are operating as a business, even before you file your LLC, you are entitled to deduct legitimate business expenses from your taxable income. The tools you bought to start. The gas you burned driving to jobs. The phone you use to book appointments and communicate with clients. The work boots on your feet. Every dollar that is a genuine business expense reduces the income you pay taxes on, and that advantage adds up over a full year of operation. Keep your receipts. Track your mileage. The IRS does not volunteer this information, which is why most people who could benefit from it never do.

Before You Launch

Get your EIN from IRS.gov before you take your first dollar. It is free and takes ten minutes, and it separates your business income from your personal income from day one. Open a separate bank account for the business. Set aside twenty to thirty percent of every payment for taxes before you spend the rest. These three steps take one afternoon and they are the difference between building something real and running an expensive hobby that gets you in trouble with the IRS two years from now.

CHAPTER 5.2

The 10 Businesses

BUSINESS #1 Mobile Car Detailing

Rich people hate dirty cars and hate driving to the car wash even more. You bring the service to them, and convenience is something they will pay a premium for every time.

STARTUP KIT

Item	Approx. Cost
Shop Vac (Home Depot or Walmart)	~$160
100ft Extension Cord	~$30
Garden Hose and Spray Nozzle	~$30
Chemical Guys Interior and Exterior Kit	~$50
Microfiber Towels (bulk pack)	~$20
Buckets, sponges, detailing brushes	~$15
TOTAL	**~$305**

THE MATH TO $100K

Daily target: $100 per full detail (interior and exterior). Three to four cars gets you to $333.

Time per job: Roughly two hours per car. Six to eight hours of work on a full day.

The note: This business scales fast because satisfied customers refer their coworkers, neighbors, and family without being asked. One good client in an office park is a gateway to the entire building.

GETTING CUSTOMERS

Go to office parks, dental offices, or apartment complexes. Walk in and offer to detail a car in the parking lot while the owner is already at work. The script is simple: 'I am detailing in the lot right now and I have an opening. I can have your car looking brand new before you leave today for a hundred dollars.' They either say yes or they do not, and the next car is ten steps away.

PRO TIP

Offer a monthly package, two details per month for a flat rate, to your best clients. Recurring revenue on a detailing business changes the entire financial model.

BUSINESS #2 Trash Can Cleaning

Everybody's garbage can smells like something died in it. Nobody wants to clean it. You do it, and you do it on a subscription so the money comes in whether or not you feel like working that day.

STARTUP KIT

Item	Approx. Cost
Used Pressure Washer (Facebook Marketplace)	~$150
Commercial Degreaser and Bleach	~$30
Long-handled scrub brush	~$15
Garden Hose	~$30
TOTAL	**~$225**

THE MATH TO $100K

Daily target: $25 per can, ten minutes per can. Thirteen to fourteen cans a day gets you to $333.

Time per job: Ten minutes per can once you have a system. The goal is a tight geographic route so you are not burning an hour driving between stops.

The note: Go to the wealthier neighborhoods on trash day. Find the cans that clearly have not been cleaned since the Obama administration. Tape a flyer directly to the lid: 'I can make this smell like lemons for $25. Text me.' The visual is the pitch.

GETTING CUSTOMERS

Do not sell one-time cleans. Sell monthly subscriptions. Twenty dollars a month, and you show up the day after trash day every single time. Build a route of two hundred to three hundred houses and you have a business that prints money on autopilot with almost no overhead.

PRO TIP

Post a before-and-after video of the nastiest can you can find. That one clip sells the whole route for you, because nobody knew this service existed until they watched the grime leave.

BUSINESS #3 Headlight Restoration

Cloudy headlights make a car look ten years older than it is and can fail a state inspection. A replacement headlight assembly runs three hundred to five hundred dollars. You fix both for sixty in twenty minutes.

STARTUP KIT

Item	Approx. Cost
Cordless Drill (Ryobi or similar)	~$60
3M Headlight Restoration Kits (bulk pack)	~$150
Painter's Tape	~$10

TOTAL	~$220

THE MATH TO $100K

Daily target: $60 per pair. Six cars gets you to $360.

Time per job: Twenty minutes per car once you know the process. Two hours of actual work to hit your daily number. The rest of the day is finding the cars.

The note: Walmart parking lots are your hunting ground. Walk the lot, find cars with yellowed or foggy headlights, and wait near the car until the owner comes out. The script: 'Hey, I noticed your headlights are pretty foggy. That is actually a safety issue in a lot of states and can fail inspection. I can restore them right here in about twenty minutes while you finish shopping. Sixty bucks.' Most people say yes because the alternative costs them five times as much at a shop.

GETTING CUSTOMERS

Partner with used car dealerships. Offer to restore headlights on their inventory at a bulk rate before they put cars on the lot. One dealership relationship can be worth thousands of dollars a month in consistent volume.

PRO TIP

Work the used-car lots and small dealers. They have twenty cars sitting there with foggy headlights killing the sale, and they will hand you all of them at once.

BUSINESS #4 Residential Window Cleaning

Homeowners ignore their windows for years. First-floor only, no tall ladders, no insurance complications, no liability nightmares. Just clean glass and a check.

STARTUP KIT

Item	Approx. Cost
Professional Squeegee and Scrubber (Ettore or Unger)	~$60
Extension pole	~$40
Bucket and Dawn dish soap	~$15
Microfiber detail towels	~$20
TOTAL	**~$135**

THE MATH TO $100K

Daily target: $150 per house, outside first-floor windows only. Two to three houses hits your daily target.

Time per job: Three to four hours per house depending on size. You can realistically do two houses in a full day when you are starting out and scale to three as you get faster.

The note: Door knock in neighborhoods where the windows are visibly dirty. Look for homes with a lot of trees nearby. Pollen and sap accumulate fast, and the owners always know it but never deal with it. The script: 'I am cleaning windows in the neighborhood today. I can do all your first-floor exterior windows for a hundred and fifty dollars. Takes me about three hours and I leave them streak-free.' Offer a seasonal package, spring and fall, to every client you land.

GETTING CUSTOMERS

Offer add-on services at the door: screen cleaning, track cleaning, and interior windows as an upgrade. A $150 job can become a $250 job with three minutes of upselling.

PRO TIP

Sell inside and outside as one price, then put the customer on a quarterly plan. Windows get dirty on a schedule, so get on that same schedule and stop hunting for the next job.

BUSINESS #5 Pooper Scooper Service

Dog owners are busy, lazy, and willing to pay someone else to deal with the part of pet ownership they hate the most. This is a volume game on a recurring subscription model.

STARTUP KIT

Item	Approx. Cost
Rake and collection pan set	~$30
Heavy duty contractor bags	~$20
Waterproof boots	~$50
Disinfectant spray for tools	~$10
TOTAL	**~$110**

THE MATH TO $100K

Daily target: $20 per visit per week. Seventeen yards per day gets you to your number.

Time per job: Ten minutes per yard on a tight route. The key is density. You want stops clustered in the same neighborhood so you are walking, not driving, between most of them.

The note: Facebook neighborhood groups are your best channel. Post this: 'I am a local entrepreneur launching a pet waste removal service in [Neighborhood Name]. The first clean is free if you sign up for a monthly plan. Text me to schedule.' The free first clean converts at a high rate because the barrier to trying it is zero.

GETTING CUSTOMERS

Build your route strategically. A tight cluster of thirty clients in one neighborhood can generate close to two thousand dollars a month in recurring revenue that takes less than a full week to service. This business is not glamorous. That is exactly why it works. Most people will not do it, which means the ones who will do not have much competition.

PRO TIP

This is the ultimate subscription. Nobody wants to do it and nobody wants to cancel it. Price it weekly, put it on autopay, and never touch a one-time job.

BUSINESS #6 Gutter Cleaning

Leaves and debris clog gutters and backed-up gutters destroy fascia boards, foundations, and basements. Homeowners know the gutters need cleaning and put it off until something breaks. You fix it before it does.

STARTUP KIT

Item	Approx. Cost

Ladder, Little Giant or quality extension (used is fine)	~$200
Heavy work gloves	~$20
Bucket and gutter scoop	~$15
TOTAL	**~$235**

THE MATH TO $100K

Daily target: $150 per house. Two to three houses hits your daily target.

Time per job: Forty-five minutes to an hour per house for a single-story home. Stick to ranch and single-story homes until you have liability insurance.

The note: Drive neighborhoods in the fall when leaves are dropping and trees are visibly overhanging rooflines. You can see which homes need the service before you ever knock. Script: 'I noticed you have some significant debris building up in your gutters, you can see it from the street. That backs up during rain and can start rotting the wood underneath. I can clear them out today for a hundred and fifty dollars.' Most homeowners know it needs to happen and are relieved someone showed up.

GETTING CUSTOMERS

Get liability insurance once you have your first few clients. It costs less than most people think and it opens you up to two-story homes, which command higher prices, and commercial properties, which are larger contracts. One property management company relationship can mean a dozen buildings.

PRO TIP

Sell it twice a year, spring and fall, and lock both visits in up front. One knock, two jobs, and you already own next season.

BUSINESS #7 Furniture Assembly

IKEA sells furniture that comes in a flat box with a forty-page instruction manual and a single Allen wrench. People buy it, bring it home, open the box, and leave it on the floor for three months. You are the person who makes it not their problem anymore.

STARTUP KIT

Item	Approx. Cost
Power drill with bit set	~$80
Hammer and rubber mallet	~$20
Full screwdriver set	~$25
Knee pads	~$20
Tape measure and level	~$15
TOTAL	**~$160**

THE MATH TO $100K

Daily target: $50 per hour or flat rate per item: $100 for a dresser, $120 for a bed frame, $150 for a wardrobe. Six to seven billable hours covers your daily target.

Time per job: Most pieces take thirty minutes to an hour once you know the systems. Flat-rate pricing rewards your speed. The faster you get, the more you make per hour without charging more.

The note: Create a profile on TaskRabbit and Thumbtack immediately. These platforms match you with people actively looking for exactly what you do. Respond within minutes to every inquiry. Response speed is one of the biggest factors in getting selected on these platforms.

GETTING CUSTOMERS

Partner with the TV mounting business below. Offer a combined service, 'I assemble your furniture and mount your TV in the same visit,' and charge a flat package rate. Two services in one appointment increases your hourly rate significantly and gives clients a reason to book you over someone who only does one thing.

PRO TIP

Camp where the furniture shows up. Get on TaskRabbit and Thumbtack, but also drop a card at every apartment leasing office in town, because new tenants with a truck full of boxes are your customer every single week.

BUSINESS #8 Sneaker Restoration

Sneaker culture moves billions of dollars a year. People spend three hundred dollars on Jordans, wear them twice, and want them looking brand new again. You make that happen.

STARTUP KIT

Item	Approx. Cost
Reshoevn8r or Jason Markk cleaning kit	~$80
Brush set (soft, medium, and stiff)	~$30
Shoe trees for shaping during cleaning	~$20

Sole whitening cream	~$20
TOTAL	**~$150**

THE MATH TO $100K

Daily target: $40 to $60 for a deep clean and sole icing. Eight to nine pairs a day hits your target.

Time per job: Batch your work. Clean nine pairs in a single session. It is far more efficient than cleaning one at a time, and the quality is consistent.

The note: Instagram is your storefront. Before-and-after photos of a cleaned pair of sneakers perform better than almost any other content in this niche because the transformation is visual and immediate. Post every single job. Tag the brands. Use the location.

GETTING CUSTOMERS

Go to your local barbershop and offer the barbers a free clean on their best pair. If a barber rocks your cleaned sneakers in the shop and someone asks about them, you just got a referral machine. The barbershop is one of the highest-trust social environments in the community. A single barber who vouches for you is worth ten social media posts.

PRO TIP

Your marketing is the before-and-after. Post every pair, tag the model, and let the sneakerheads find you. One clean pair of retros in your feed is worth a hundred flyers.

BUSINESS #9 Moving Helper — Labor Only

People rent the U-Haul and then realize they cannot get the couch down the stairs by themselves. You are not a moving company. You are the muscle they should have booked before they rented the truck.

STARTUP KIT

Item	Approx. Cost
Back brace (quality one, not cheap)	~$30
Grip gloves	~$20
Forearm Forklift moving straps	~$30
TOTAL	**~$80**

THE MATH TO $100K

Daily target: $50 per hour solo, $100 per hour with a partner. Six to seven hours solo or three and a half hours with a partner gets you to your number.

Time per job: Moving jobs run long and they run physical. Bring water, wear the back brace, and use the straps. Your body is your equipment in this business and you cannot work if it breaks.

The note: Post near U-Haul locations: flyers in the parking lot, a listing on Craigslist and Facebook Marketplace in the services section, and a profile on TaskRabbit. People search for moving help the same day they need it, so be visible and be available.

GETTING CUSTOMERS

Bring a reliable partner and split the rate. At one hundred dollars per hour for the pair, a four-hour move pays each of you two hundred dollars for an afternoon of work. Build a small network of two or three people you trust so you can take larger jobs and handle multiple bookings on the same day.

PRO TIP

Partner with the truck rental spots and the apartment complexes. People rent the truck first and then realize they have nobody to lift. Be the name the counter hands them.

BUSINESS #10 TV Mounting

People buy sixty-five-inch televisions and are genuinely afraid to drill into their wall. They need someone confident, fast, and clean, and they will pay well for it.

STARTUP KIT

Item	Approx. Cost
Quality stud finder	~$50
Drill with assorted bits	~$80
Socket set	~$30
Level and tape measure	~$20
TOTAL	**~$180**

THE MATH TO $100K

Daily target: $100 to $150 per mount. Two to three installs gets you past your daily target.

Time per job: Forty-five minutes per mount once you have done a few. The job is fast. The value to the customer is high. The margin is excellent.

The note: Search Facebook Marketplace for people buying or selling large televisions. Message the sellers:

'Do you offer mounting with delivery?' Message the buyers: 'Congrats on the new TV, do you have someone to mount it or do you need a hand?' You are fishing in a pond where every single person has a fish.

GETTING CUSTOMERS

Upsell wire concealment on every single job. Running the cables through the wall so nothing is visible adds ten minutes and fifty extra dollars to the invoice. Almost everyone says yes when you show them what it looks like. That upsell alone can add fifteen to twenty thousand dollars to your annual revenue without adding a single new client.

PRO TIP

Upsell the wire concealment and the soundbar mount every time. The mount is the reason they called. The clean, hidden wires are what they will happily pay double for.

CHAPTER 5.3

Blueprint in Action — A Real Story

"The blueprint only works if you work it. Here is proof."

Everything in this book is based on real principles that produce real results, and the following is a composite profile drawn from real people who followed these steps. The names and identifying details have been changed but the numbers and the timeline and the decisions are real.

SUCCESS PROFILE

Marcus T. (name changed for privacy)

Age at start: 26

Starting credit score: 581

Starting income: $34,000 per year as a warehouse supervisor

Starting business capital: $0

Starting financial knowledge: Had never heard the term utilization rate

Month 1 — The Foundation

Marcus pulled his credit reports for the first time and found three errors, two accounts with incorrect balances and one collection that did not belong to him, and he filed disputes on all three the same week. He opened a secured card with a two-hundred-dollar deposit and linked it to his Netflix subscription and set it to auto-pay in full. He also filed his LLC and got his EIN the same week at zero cost, then opened a business checking account at a local credit union. He started taking furniture assembly jobs on TaskRabbit on weekends and putting every dollar into the business account. He did not feel like anything was happening and nothing visible had changed and he kept going anyway.

Month 3 — First Movement

The credit disputes resolved and all three errors were corrected and the secured card had three months of perfect history reporting, and his score moved from 581 to 634. He requested to be added as an authorized user on his mother's oldest credit card and within thirty days his score moved to 668. His weekend revenue from furniture assembly and TV mounting was averaging eleven hundred dollars a month and he had calculated his Freedom Number and was working toward it.

Month 12 — The Number Changed

By month twelve Marcus's side business was generating an average of twenty-two hundred dollars a month and his credit score sat at 731 and he had five thousand dollars in his business account and three thousand in personal savings. He had not quit his job yet, but he had given himself a six-month target to hit his Freedom Number. The person who started this journey twelve months earlier with a 581 score and zero business capital was no longer the same person holding the pen.

Marcus did not do anything extraordinary. He had no unique skill set and no large network and no startup capital. What he had was consistency and a willingness to make decisions that served his future self instead of his present comfort. The blueprint works. The only variable is whether you work it.

CHAPTER 5.4

The Mindset of the Weekend Warrior

Every business on this list has one thing in common: it starts with a decision and ends with execution. There is no planning phase that makes the first job easier. There is no research that substitutes for the experience of showing up to a stranger's house with your equipment and doing the work. The learning happens in the field, and the only way to get to the field is to stop preparing to go and actually go.

The biggest trap for people at this stage is mistaking activity for progress. Creating a logo is not progress. Designing a business card is not progress. Spending three weekends researching which pressure washer to buy while the season passes is not progress. Progress is a paid invoice. Progress is a repeat customer. Progress is the fourth job in a week when the first three gave you the confidence to ask for referrals.

Momentum is real and it compounds in both directions. Every day you do not start, the mental barrier to starting gets slightly higher. Every day you do work, even one job, even a small one, the barrier drops and the confidence builds. The people who build successful businesses from nothing are not the ones who waited until they felt ready. They are the ones who went before they were ready and figured out the details in motion.

You do not need a perfect website. You do not need a truck wrap or a uniform or a business card with embossed letters. You need a phone number, a way to accept payment (Cash App, Venmo, Zelle, Square), and enough equipment to do the job. Every dollar you make above expenses in the first ninety days goes into two places: reinvestment into the business and savings for your first real asset. Not clothes. Not going out. Not upgrading something that does not need upgrading. The business and the asset.

One more thing: tell people what you do. Every single person in your orbit should know what service you offer and how to reach you. That means family, friends, your barber, your church, neighbors, and the coworkers at the job you are still working while you build this. Word of mouth is the most powerful marketing channel available to a service business, and it costs nothing except the willingness to talk about what you are building without being embarrassed about where it is starting.

Every large company started as a small one. Every empire started as a weekend hustle. The only question that matters right now is whether you are going to be one of the people who starts or one of the people who watches someone else start and wishes they had when they had the chance.

You have the chance right now.

—Joseph Grimes

PART SIX

The Sales Blueprint

From the Street to the Boardroom: How to Sell Anything to Anyone

"You are always selling. If you are not selling a product, you are selling yourself. Learn the game."

We started this book with a twelve-year-old running a backpack operation. We built the mindset, the credit, the financial literacy, the business structure, and the side hustle. And now we are here, the last section, the one that ties every single piece of this Arsenal together, because none of it works without this.

You cannot get a job without selling yourself in an interview. You cannot get a loan without selling a banker on your creditworthiness. You cannot get customers without selling your service. You cannot lead a team without selling your vision. You cannot raise your kids to be disciplined without selling them on why it matters. Every meaningful outcome in your life required you to convince another human being of something, and the quality of your life is directly proportional to how good you are at doing that.

Sales is not a job title. It is a life skill, and the people who treat it as optional are the ones who spend their careers waiting to be discovered instead of going out and getting what they came for.

CHAPTER 6.1

The Origin Story

I have been selling since I was twelve years old and I never once called it sales until I was doing it professionally.

It started with Pokémon cards and lollipops out of my backpack at school. I figured out early that certain cards moved faster than others, that pricing mattered, and that if I made the transaction feel easy and fun, the same kids came back the next day. I was not reading sales books. I was paying attention to what worked, iterating on what did not, and building a customer base out of my peers before I was old enough to have a work permit.

Then came the suburban candy hustle, getting picked up from my neighborhood and dropped off in wealthy subdivisions to sell door-to-door with a group of other kids. That version of selling was a different animal entirely. These were strangers. Adults. People with no reason to open their door and certainly no reason to hand cash to a kid they had never seen before. I had seconds. Not minutes. Seconds to establish enough trust, enough warmth, enough presence that the door stayed open instead of closing in my face.

Some doors closed anyway. A lot of them, honestly. And I learned something in that experience that no classroom has ever taught effectively: rejection does not mean what you think it means. A closed door is not a verdict. It is a data point. It tells you something about that particular person at that particular moment, and it tells you nothing about whether the next door will open. The rookies treated every no like a personal injury. The ones who made money treated every no like a step closer to the next yes.

I carried those instincts into Verizon Wireless, a Fortune 50 company, and they translated immediately. The technology was different. The price points were different. The stakes were higher. But the human psychology on the other side of the transaction was identical. People buy from people they trust. People buy solutions to problems they have already identified. People buy when they feel understood, not when they feel pitched at. I became a top performer, then a sales leader, then a mentor to other reps, and every principle I taught came from a suburban doorstep at fourteen years old.

The principles do not change. The context does. That is what makes sales the most transferable skill you will ever develop.

CHAPTER 6.2

The Mindset

"Sales is the only profession where you can fail ninety percent of the time and still be a millionaire."

If you are afraid of hearing no, you are not ready to sell anything to anyone. That is not an insult. It is a diagnosis, and it is fixable. But until you fix it, every other skill in this section is going to be limited by the fact that you will unconsciously avoid the moments that matter most because those are the moments where rejection is possible.

Rejection is not failure. Rejection is armor. Every no you collect makes the next no easier to absorb, and at some point the armor gets thick enough that the no stops carrying any emotional weight at all. It is just information. It means that person, in that moment, was not the right fit or the right time, and your job is to move to the next one without carrying the last one with you.

The Biology of the Problem

Humans are biologically wired to avoid social rejection. Thousands of years of evolution have programmed us to seek belonging and to experience exclusion as a genuine threat. Being told no by a stranger triggers the same neural pathway as being excluded from a social group, which is why it feels disproportionately bad and why so many people will do almost anything to avoid it, including not asking for the sale.

Knowing this does not make the wiring go away. But it gives you something to work with. When you feel the discomfort of potential rejection, you can recognize it for what it is, a biological response to a perceived social threat, rather than a signal to stop. The discomfort is not telling you that you are doing something wrong. It is telling you that you are doing something that matters. Go toward it.

The Freedom on the Other Side

There is a specific kind of freedom that comes from genuinely not caring what people think about you, and sales is one of the fastest paths to it. Once you have heard no enough times, once you have been hung up on and dismissed and ignored enough times and kept going anyway, the social anxiety that holds most people back from asking for what they want starts to lose its grip. You realize the worst thing that can happen is a stranger says no and life continues unchanged, and that realization is liberating in ways that extend far beyond the sales floor.

The people who are most free in their personal and professional lives are the ones who learned to detach their self-worth from other people's responses. Sales teaches you that faster than almost anything else, if you let it.

CHAPTER 6.3

The Math

"Sales is not magic. It is math. If you are broke, it is because you did not talk to enough people."

Talent matters less in sales than almost any other high-earning profession. What matters is volume, and volume is entirely within your control regardless of how naturally gifted you are at the craft.

Every salesperson operates with a close rate, a percentage of the people they talk to who ultimately buy. A good closer might convert thirty percent of qualified prospects. An exceptional one might hit fifty. A beginner might start at ten or fifteen. The exact number is less important than understanding the implication: if your close rate is ten percent and you want ten sales, you need to talk to one hundred people. Not fifty. Not sixty. One hundred.

Most people who struggle in sales are not bad closers. They are low-volume prospectors who are trying to make ten conversations do the work of one hundred. And because each conversation carries more psychological weight when there are only ten of them, the pressure shows up in the interaction and tanks the conversion rate further. High volume takes the pressure off. When you know there are ninety-nine more conversations behind this one, you relax, and relaxed salespeople close more.

The Funnel

Step 1 — Prospecting: How many people did you reach out to today?

Step 2 — Appointments: How many agreed to hear what you have to offer?

Step 3 — Presentations: How many actually saw the full offer?

Step 4 — The Close: How many paid?

Work backward from your income goal to your daily prospecting number and treat that number like a non-negotiable. Not a goal. A minimum. The close is where the money is, but prospecting is where the close comes from, and the salesperson who controls their prospecting activity controls their income regardless of what the market is doing.

Track Everything

The best sales leaders I worked with did not manage by motivation or pep talks. They managed by data. They knew their team's numbers, calls made, appointments set, presentations delivered, deals closed, and they could diagnose a performance problem from those numbers before it ever showed up in a paycheck. When you know your numbers, you know exactly what to fix. When you do not, you are guessing, and guessing is expensive.

Track your activity every single day. Not just your results. Your activity. Because results lag behind activity by days or weeks. If you only track results, you will not know the pipeline is empty until it shows up in your revenue, and by then it is already too late to fix it quickly.

CHAPTER 6.4

The Vibe

"It is not what you say. It is how you say it. Your tone is closing deals before your words even start."

Research by Dr. Albert Mehrabian on communication effectiveness breaks down how people receive messages in face-to-face interactions. The numbers are instructive even if you have heard them before.

Component	Weight in Communication
Body language and physical presence	55%
Tonality, how you sound	38%
The actual words you use	7%

In practice, the script matters far less than most salespeople think, and the way you carry yourself matters far more. A mediocre script delivered with certainty and warmth outperforms a perfect script delivered with hesitation every single time. Your voice, your posture, your eye contact, and your energy are doing most of the selling before a single word of your pitch is spoken.

Mirroring

People buy from people who are like them. This is not a theory. It is a documented psychological principle called the similarity-attraction effect, and you can use it deliberately. If the person you are talking to speaks quickly, match their pace. If they lean back in their chair, give them space and ease your own posture. If they are warm and conversational, be warm and conversational. If they are direct and businesslike, tighten up and get to the point.

Mirroring is not mimicry. It is calibration. You are reading the person in front of you and adapting your communication style to meet them where they are. The result is that they feel understood without knowing why, which lowers their defenses and makes them more receptive to everything that comes after it.

Tonality

Sound certain. This sounds simple and it is the thing most salespeople get wrong. If your voice goes up at the end of a statement, making it sound like a question, you are telegraphing doubt, and doubt is contagious. State your price with a flat, even tone. Describe your product with conviction. Answer objections without flinching. Certainty is not aggression. It is the calm confidence of someone who knows what they have and knows it is worth buying.

Your tonality on price is especially important. If you sound uncomfortable when you say the number, if there is any hesitation, any apologetic quality, any upward inflection, the customer hears it and becomes uncertain themselves. Practice saying your price out loud until it comes out the same way you would say your own name. No drama, no apology, no question mark at the end.

Humor as a Pattern Interrupt

When you make someone laugh, their defenses drop. Humor creates a moment of genuine human connection that does not coexist with the skeptical, transactional headspace most people bring into a sales interaction. You do not need to be a comedian. You need to be a human being who is not so focused on closing that you forget to connect. A well-timed, self-aware comment about the situation, a light observation about something in the room, a moment of genuine levity, any of these can shift the energy of a conversation and make the person in front of you feel like they are talking to a person rather than a pitch.

CHAPTER 6.5

The Discovery

"Prescription without diagnosis is malpractice. Find the pain before you name the price."

The single biggest mistake people make when they start selling is pitching immediately. Someone expresses the slightest interest and the rookie launches into everything the product does, every feature, every benefit, every reason it is the best option on the market, before they have asked a single question about what the person actually needs.

This approach fails because it treats every customer as the same person with the same problem. In reality every customer has a specific situation with a specific pain point, and your job is to find that pain point before you position your solution against it. The product does not close the deal. The alignment between the product and a problem the customer already recognizes does.

The Doctor Frame

Think about how a doctor operates. A patient comes in with a symptom and the doctor does not immediately hand them a prescription. They ask questions. They do an examination. They gather information until they understand what is actually happening, and then they prescribe the specific solution for that specific condition. A doctor who prescribed before diagnosing would be committing malpractice.

Sales works the same way. You are the doctor. Your product or service is the prescription. And the discovery conversation, the questions you ask before you pitch anything, is the examination. Skip the examination and everything that comes after it is guesswork.

The Wrong Way and the Right Way

Customer: *My phone battery dies all the time.*

Rookie: *This phone has an amazing battery, forty-eight hours on a single charge!*

Pro: *That is frustrating. How does that affect your day when it happens?*

The rookie took the surface complaint and pitched at it. The pro went deeper, because the battery is not the real problem. The real problem is whatever the dead battery is costing the customer. Maybe it is missed calls from a client. Maybe it is anxiety when they travel. Maybe it is embarrassment in meetings. Find the real problem and you have found the sale.

The One-Layer-Deeper Rule

When a customer gives you a complaint or a concern, your first response should almost never be a solution. It should be a follow-up question that goes one layer deeper into the problem. 'How does that affect you?' and 'What happens when that occurs?' and 'Tell me more about that situation' are your most powerful discovery tools, and they cost nothing except the discipline to use them before you pitch.

The customer who mentions a dead battery and then tells you they missed a critical client call because of it, and that it cost them a relationship, is not buying a phone. They are buying peace of mind, professional reliability, and the confidence that this specific problem will not happen again. Sell them that. The phone is just the vehicle.

CHAPTER 6.6

The Pitch

"People do not buy products. They buy solutions to problems they have already told you about."

By the time you get to the pitch, the customer has already done most of the work. They have told you what is wrong, what it costs them, and what they wish were different. Your job in the pitch is not to introduce new information. It is to connect the solution you have directly to the problem they just described, in their language, using the specific details they gave you.

This is called value positioning, and it is what separates a presentation that lands from one that slides off. When you say 'you mentioned that you travel for work and cannot afford to have your phone die on you. This device has a forty-eight-hour battery life, which means the next time you are in back-to-back meetings or on a long flight, you never have to think about it,' you are not selling a battery. You are selling the solution to a problem they told you was real. That alignment is what closes.

Tie Every Feature to Their Specific Pain

Features without context are just specifications on a sheet. Nobody gets emotionally connected to a specification. They get emotionally connected to what that specification does for their life. The forty-eight-hour battery is a feature. 'You will never miss another client call because your phone died' is a benefit that speaks directly to the pain they described. Always bridge the feature to the benefit, and always make the benefit personal to what they told you in discovery.

The Convenience Factor

People are busy and they are lazy, and that is not a criticism. It is a fact about human behavior that good salespeople use to their advantage. The harder it is to buy from you, the fewer people will. The easier you make the transaction, the more of them follow through.

Remove every friction point you can identify. If you can set it up for them, offer to set it up. If you can deliver it, deliver it. If you can handle the paperwork, handle the paperwork. 'I can have this ready and running for you before you leave today' is more powerful than any feature you could describe, because it tells the customer that buying from you requires almost nothing from them except a yes. Make it easy to say yes and harder to justify saying no.

Paint the Picture

Before you ask for the close, give the customer a moment to see themselves on the other side of the purchase. Walk them through what using your product or service looks and feels like once the transaction is done. 'Imagine you get to the airport tomorrow and your phone is at full charge when you land, without thinking about it once during the flight.' That sentence is not a feature and it is not a benefit. It is a scene. And people buy scenes. They buy the version of their life where the problem is solved, and your job is to make that version vivid enough that the current version becomes unacceptable by comparison.

CHAPTER 6.7

The Close

"The only bad close is the one you did not ask for."

You did the discovery. You built the pitch around their specific pain. You painted the picture. Everything is aligned and the customer is nodding and you can feel that they are there, and then you hesitate. You do not ask. You keep talking, adding more information, filling the silence with features they do not need, because asking for the money feels pushy and you do not want to push.

That hesitation is costing you deals every single day. The close is not pushy. The close is the logical conclusion of everything that came before it. You found the problem. You showed them the solution. You built the value. At this point, not asking for the sale is doing them a disservice, because the solution exists and you have already demonstrated that it fits their need. The only thing standing between them and the outcome they said they wanted is your willingness to ask.

The Assumptive Close

The assumptive close is built on a simple psychological principle: when you behave as though the decision has already been made, the customer's brain often agrees with you. Instead of 'Would you like to move forward?', which invites a binary yes-or-no decision, you ask a question that assumes yes and simply determines the details.

Wrong: *So would you like to go ahead and buy it?*

Right: *Do you want to put this on the card on file or use a new one?*

The first question puts the customer in a decision frame. The second one puts them in a details frame. The decision is assumed, and they are simply choosing how. This is not manipulation. The customer always has the ability to say they are not ready. But framing the close assumptively removes the psychological barrier of the yes-or-no moment and makes it easier for a decided customer to move forward without overthinking it.

The Silence Trick

After you close, stop talking. Completely. The first person to speak after the close loses, and if that person is you, you have given the customer a reason to reconsider by filling the silence with nervous energy or unnecessary information. Ask for the money, then be quiet and let the moment breathe.

The silence will feel longer than it is. It will feel uncomfortable. That discomfort is mutual. The customer feels it too, and the resolution to mutual discomfort is for someone to speak. If you let it be them, what they say is usually yes or an objection you can work with. Either outcome is better than you talking yourself out of a sale that was already yours.

Handling Objections

An objection is not a no. It is a request for more information presented in the form of resistance. 'It is too expensive' means 'you have not yet shown me that the value exceeds the cost.' 'I need to think about it' means 'I am not yet convinced enough to decide right now.' 'I want to check with my spouse' sometimes means exactly that and sometimes means 'I need a socially acceptable exit because something is still not resolved for me.'

The response to any objection is a question, not a counter-argument. 'What specifically would you want to think through?' 'What would make the price feel right for what you are getting?' 'If your spouse agreed, is this something you would want to move forward with?' These questions surface what is actually blocking the close so you can address the real concern rather than arguing against the stated one.

Common Objection	The Right Response
It's too expensive.	'What would the price need to be for this to feel like the right value?'
I need to think about it.	'Absolutely. What specifically do you want to think through?'
I want to shop around.	'That makes sense. What would you be looking for in a comparison?'
I need to talk to my spouse.	'Of course. If they are on board, is this something you would want?'
Now is not a good time.	'I understand. When would be a better time to revisit this?'

CHAPTER 6.8

The Why

"Motivation is garbage. Discipline is reliable. Find your why and let the why run on discipline."

External motivation is real and it is worthless. A bonus check gets you fired up for a week and then life normalizes and the fire goes out. A leaderboard keeps you competitive until you fall off the top and then the same leaderboard becomes a source of discouragement. A manager who inspires you eventually leaves, gets promoted, or has a bad week themselves, and suddenly the thing that was driving you is gone.

Internal motivation is different because it does not depend on anything outside of you. It is the reason that is still standing when the external rewards disappear, when the recognition dries up, when the season is slow and the pipeline is cold and showing up feels pointless. It is the thing you are ultimately building toward, and it is the only fuel source reliable enough to run a sales career on.

Find Your Actual Why

Not the why that sounds good in a meeting. The one that is true. For me it was proving to myself that I could outwork everyone in the room. Not to beat them, but because I needed to know what I was capable of, and the only way to find out was to push past every comfortable limit and see what was on the other side. That was the thing that got me out of bed when the quota felt impossible and kept me on the floor when everyone else went to lunch.

Yours might be providing a life for your kids that looks nothing like the one you had. It might be buying your mother a house. It might be proving someone wrong who told you you were not capable. It might be the specific version of freedom you have imagined so many times it feels almost real. Whatever it is, it needs to be specific enough to picture clearly, emotional enough to move you, and true enough that it holds up under pressure.

Write it down. Keep it somewhere you see it when the motivation is gone and the discipline is all you have left. Because there will be days when the discipline is all you have left, and on those days the why is the only thing standing between you and quitting something that would have paid off if you had stayed.

The Self-Reflection Loop

The best salespeople I have ever worked with shared one habit: they reviewed their own performance without ego. After every call, every presentation, every interaction: what went well, what did not, what would they do differently, and what does that difference tell them about their current gaps. This loop runs continuously and it compounds over time into a level of skill that looks like natural talent to people who never saw the process behind it.

Iterate. Self-reflect. Double down on what works. Cut what does not. The sales profession rewards the people who treat themselves like a product in beta, always collecting feedback, always improving, never finished.

CHAPTER 6.9

Sales as a Life Skill

We are at the end of this book and I want to close with something that goes beyond the sales floor, because everything we have covered in these six sections ultimately comes back to this.

When I was twelve years old selling Pokémon cards out of my backpack, I was not thinking about a career in sales. I was not thinking about Fortune 50 companies or MBA programs or investment portfolios. I was thinking about what I wanted and how to get it, and I figured out fast that getting it required convincing other people that the trade was worth it for them too. That is the whole game. That has always been the whole game.

Everything in this Arsenal required you to sell something. The Accountability Gap asked you to sell yourself on a harder story about your own life, one where you are the variable, not the victim. The credit section asked you to sell yourself on delayed gratification and disciplined behavior over the course of months. The financial literacy section asked you to sell yourself on thinking like an owner instead of an employee. The business launchpad asked you to sell your vision to a bank, a landlord, a first customer who had no reason to trust you yet. The $400 Startup asked you to walk up to strangers and convince them to hand you cash for a service you were delivering for the first time.

Every one of those moments was a sale. The only question was whether you were skilled enough to close it.

The skills in this section work in every context where a human being is trying to influence another human being toward a decision. Which means they work in your career, your relationships, your parenting, your negotiations, your advocacy, and every other arena where the outcome depends on more than just your individual effort. You will need to persuade someone for the rest of your life. You might as well be exceptional at it.

Go back through your days and identify every moment where a better outcome was available and you did not get it because you did not ask, did not communicate the value clearly, or let the discomfort of the close make the decision for you. Those moments are the gap between where you are and where you could be, and they close the same way every other gap in this book closes, through knowledge, practice, and the willingness to keep going when it does not work the first time.

This book started with a kid in a backpack and it ends with a complete system for anyone who is done waiting for someone else to hand them the life they want. The Arsenal is loaded. Every weapon is in your hands. The only thing left to do is use them.

Iterate. Self-reflect. Double down.

Go get the bag.

—Joseph Grimes

CONCLUSION

The Arsenal Never Closes

"The wealth gap will not close itself. The knowledge gap will not close itself. That is your job now."

You made it to the end of this book, which already puts you ahead of most people who picked it up with good intentions and put it down when the first chapter made them uncomfortable. That discomfort was not a warning to stop. It was the book working.

What you just read is not a collection of theories from someone who studied success from the outside. It is a blueprint drawn from a real life, from a kid in Orlando with no financial inheritance, no blueprint, and no safety net. A kid who decided that the absence of those things was not a reason to lose but a reason to learn faster than everyone who had them. Everything in these pages has been lived, tested, failed at, adjusted, and figured out the hard way so that you do not have to.

But a blueprint is only as valuable as the person holding it. You can have the most detailed architectural plan ever drawn and still never build the house if you never pick up a tool. This book is the plan. The tools are your time, your attention, your discipline, and your willingness to do uncomfortable things consistently over a long enough period that the results become undeniable.

Let me tell you what I want for you, because I have been specific about everything else in this book and I am going to be specific about this too.

I want you to close the Accountability Gap and stop outsourcing the responsibility for your life to circumstances you cannot control. The circumstances are real. Your response to them is more real. The gap between where you are and where you want to be closes from the inside out, and it starts with the decision to stop explaining it and start attacking it.

I want you to have a credit score above 700 within the next twelve months and to never again pay the high-interest tax that comes with letting that number sit below it. The steps are in this book. They are not complicated. They require discipline and patience and nothing else. You have both.

I want you to understand money at the level the wealthy do, not as something you earn and spend, but as something you deploy to build assets that generate more money while you sleep. The rules of the wealthy are not secret. They are just not taught in the schools most of us went to, which is why most of us graduate financially illiterate into a system designed to profit from that illiteracy. You are no longer financially illiterate.

I want you to file your LLC, open your business account, and take your first customer before you feel ready. You will not feel ready. Nobody does. The readiness comes from doing the thing, not from preparing to do it, and every day you wait is a day of revenue, experience, and momentum that does not come back.

I want you to look at a pressure washer or a set of hand tools or a shop vac and see not a piece of equipment but a pathway. A four-hundred-dollar investment that, worked correctly and consistently, generates a hundred thousand dollars a year. It asks nothing from you except your time, your effort, and your refusal to quit when it gets hard.

And I want you to learn to sell. Not just products. Yourself. Your ideas. Your vision. Your worth. Because the single most consistent factor I have seen in people who build real lives from nothing is their willingness to walk into rooms where they are not expected and make a case for why they belong there. Then keep making that case until someone says yes.

The Savage Arsenal is not just a book title. It is a description of what you now carry. Six weapons, fully loaded: mindset, credit, financial literacy, business structure, startup capital, and the ability to sell. Any one of them alone changes something in your life. All six together change the trajectory.

I did not write this book for people who have everything figured out. I wrote it for the person who has been doing everything they know how to do and still feels like they are running in place, because the problem was never their effort. It was the missing information that turns effort into momentum. You now have that information.

The system was not built for you. Build your own system. The knowledge gap was real. You have closed it. The blueprint was never handed to you. You are holding it.

What you do next is entirely up to you, and that is the point. It has always been up to you. The Arsenal just makes sure that when you decide to move, you are not moving unarmed.

Stay intentional. Stay accountable. Stay building.

—Joseph Grimes

Author · Sales Leader · Everyday Hustler

MASTER TOOL INDEX

"A weapon you cannot find when you need it is not a weapon. It is a decoration."

Every tool, framework, script, and resource in this book, on one page, so you can find it fast when the moment calls for it. The number in parentheses is the chapter it lives in. Do not just read these once. Come back and use them.

PART ONE — THE ACCOUNTABILITY GAP

Locus of Control: the difference between believing life happens to you and believing you drive it (1.1).

The Mirror Audit: sit down with no distractions and write down everything off track and your part in it (1.6).

The Language Shift: kill "I have to" and replace it with "I choose to" until you believe it (1.6).

The Delayed Gratification Drill: train the muscle that picks the future reward over the easy one (1.6).

The Circle Audit: get honest about who is pulling you forward and who is anchoring you in place (1.6).

PART TWO — THE 700 CREDIT SCORE BLUEPRINT

The Score Breakdown: the five factors and exactly what each one is worth (2.1).

The Three Golden Rules: the Phantom Limit, the Power of One, and Auto-Pay Everything (2.2).

The Ghost: how to build credit from a score of zero (2.3).

The Fixer: the 600 to 700 climb, including the Authorized User Hack, attacking balances, and disputing errors (2.4).

The Flex: the 700 to 800 push (2.5).

The Safe Starter Pack: the exact first cards and accounts to open (2.6).

The Templates: the Pay for Delete script and the Dispute Letter, ready to copy (2.7).

PART THREE — FINANCIAL LITERACY SIMPLIFIED

The Five Rules: Assets vs. Liabilities (3.2), Cash Flow is King (3.3), Credit as a Tool (3.4), Sweat Equity (3.5), and the Tax Cheat Code (3.6).

The Infinite Banking Move: borrowing against your own money instead of the bank's (3.7).

The Blueprint: the four phases, Stabilization, Acquisition, Optimization, and Liberation (3.8).

PART FOUR — THE 10-STEP BUSINESS LAUNCHPAD

The 10 Steps: the EIN (4.2), the LLC (4.3), Licenses (4.4), the Business Bank Account (4.5), Funding and Credit (4.6), the Skill Stack (4.7), Marketing (4.8), the Discipline Gap (4.9), Ten Industries Worth Your Time (4.10), and the Free Resource List (4.11).

The Free Resource List: SCORE.org, SBA.gov, IRS.gov, your local library, Canva, and DNB.com (4.11).

PART FIVE — THE $400 STARTUP

The $333 Rule: the daily number that turns any of these into a six-figure business (5.1).

The 10 Businesses: ten startups you can launch for around $400, each with a startup kit and the math to $100K (5.2).

Blueprint in Action: a real 12-month case, 581 to 731, from zero capital (5.3).

PART SIX — THE SALES BLUEPRINT

The Funnel: the four numbers you track every day, Prospecting, Appointments, Presentations, and the Close (6.3).

The Vibe: Mirroring, Tonality, and Humor as a Pattern Interrupt (6.4).

The Doctor Frame: diagnose before you prescribe (6.5).

The One-Layer-Deeper Rule: the follow-up question that finds the real pain (6.5).

The Assumptive Close: closing the sale without ever asking the awkward question (6.7).

The Silence Trick: say your number and shut up (6.7).

Handling Objections: turning "no" and "let me think about it" into a next step (6.7).

The Follow-Up Framework: the money that lives in the follow-up most people skip (6.7b).

Find Your Actual Why: the fuel that keeps you prospecting when it stops being fun (6.8).

The Self-Reflection Loop: iterate, self-reflect, double down (6.9).

BACK MATTER

Your Freedom Number Worksheet: define what free actually costs and reverse-engineer it into a daily target.

YOUR FREEDOM NUMBER WORKSHEET

"Freedom is not a feeling. It is a number. Once you know it, you can hunt it."

Everybody says they want to be free. Almost nobody can tell you what free actually costs. That is the whole problem. You cannot hit a target you have never defined, so you stay on the treadmill guessing, working hard with no finish line in sight. This worksheet gives you the finish line.

Your Freedom Number is the amount your hustle has to bring in every month so you can walk away from the job that owns your time and still keep the lights on and the life you actually want. There are two versions of it, and you need both.

The Survival Number is the floor. It is what it costs to keep breathing indoors with the power on. Rent or mortgage, utilities, food, transportation, insurance, phone, the minimum payments on your debt, and childcare if you have kids. Nothing fun. Just the bill to exist.

The Freedom Number is the Survival Number plus three things most people forget until the bill shows up: the taxes you now owe as your own boss, the money you reinvest and save so the business does not eat itself, and the actual life you are working for. Add those on top or the number is a lie.

Fill this out with real numbers, not the numbers you wish were true. The math only works if you are honest.

STEP 1 — YOUR SURVIVAL NUMBER (MONTHLY)

Housing (rent or mortgage): $________

Utilities (power, water, gas): $________

Food and household: $________

Transportation (car note, gas, insurance, transit): $________

Health insurance and medical: $________

Phone and internet: $________

Childcare and dependents: $________

Debt minimums (cards, loans): $________

Everything else you actually pay: $________

Survival Number (add it up): $________

STEP 2 — YOUR FREEDOM NUMBER (MONTHLY)

Start with your Survival Number: $________

Taxes to set aside (use 25 to 30 percent of what you earn): $________

Savings and reinvestment (pay yourself and the business first): $________

The life you are actually building (travel, giving, the things that make it worth it): $________

Freedom Number (add it up): $________

STEP 3 — TURN THE NUMBER INTO A DAILY TARGET

A number you cannot break into daily action is just a wish. Do this math.

Freedom Number divided by your average sale or job equals the jobs you need per month: ________

Jobs per month divided by the days you actually work equals jobs per day: ________

Now you are not chasing "someday." You are chasing a number you can count on your fingers before lunch. That is the difference between a dream and a plan.

THE POINT

Most people never do this because the number scares them. Do it anyway. A scary number you can see is a hundred times better than a comfortable fog you cannot. The moment you know your Freedom Number, every dollar you make has a job and every day has a target. That is when the hustle stops being noise and starts being a countdown.

Write your Freedom Number here and put this page where you will see it every morning: $________

—Joseph Grimes

ABOUT THE AUTHOR

"The mentor I never had, for the generation that needs one."

Joseph Grimes grew up in Orlando, Florida, in a neighborhood where the blueprint for financial freedom was not passed down at the dinner table. He figured it out the hard way: selling candy out of a backpack at 12, knocking on doors in rich suburbs as a teenager, climbing to top performer at a Fortune 50 company. He earned his MBA, bought his first home at 24, and built 3 businesses from the ground up.

The Savage Arsenal is not his first book and it will not be his last. His mission is simple: give the next generation the information he had to find himself, clearly, honestly, and without gatekeeping.

Stay connected and keep building:

@grimetimeready — All Platforms

www.grimetimeready.com

www.ingramcontent.com/pod-product-compliance
Lightning Source LLC
LaVergne TN
LVHW100327210926
848480LV00003B/1283

* 9 7 9 8 9 9 5 4 4 8 2 4 2 *